The GOD We Love & Serve

ALLEN DALE CURRY

GREAT COMMISSION
PUBLICATIONS

ISBN 0-934688-65-6

Copyright © 1991 by Great Commission Publications, Inc.

Second printing 2001

Printed in USA

Published by Great Commission Publications
3640 Windsor Park Drive
Suwanee, GA 30024-3897

Table of Contents

To Marilyn:

"A wife of noble character…
She is worth far more
than rubies.
Her husband has
full confidence in her…"
(Prov. 31:10, 11)

Introduction

This book has a twofold objective. The first is to examine some of the characteristics of God. For it is important for all Christians to *understand* something about who God is, to be acquainted with his character and nature.

There will be no attempt to be comprehensive, however. Instead of trying to catalog the numerous aspects of God's character, we will examine only a few of them. To a certain extent the selection of topics is arbitrary, but I hope you will not be put off by this. Since this is a short book, perhaps it can serve as a brief introduction to the study of the doctrine of God.

The second objective of this book is to demonstrate that we must *respond* to God. That is the reason for the title, *The God We Love and Serve*. Under the rubrics of loving and serving God, we will look at the many ways in which we can please him. He is not some unknown, meaningless being, or an abstract idea that religious people talk about. Rather, he is a personal God who demands that we respond to him.

The Scriptures themselves are filled with examples of people's lives being changed because of their encounters with God. I hope that, as you study this book, you also will experience similar changes. Perhaps as you study about God, you will find yourself loving him more and serving him more effectively. That is certainly my hope and prayer.

ALLEN D. CURRY
Reformed Theological Seminary
Jackson, Mississippi

God Is:
The Proper Perspective

* God exists!

AT THE END OF A LONG DAY OF DRIVING in the western part of the United States, I was anxious to get to my destination. As I approached the crest of one of the foothills of the Rocky Mountains, I saw the highway that would take me on the final part of my journey laid out just ahead of me—or so I thought.

When I reached the top of the rise, I could see that the road I was on snaked back and forth for miles before it reached the highway. I was disappointed—I wasn't as near to my destination as I had thought. I realized I would have to drive many more miles than I had anticipated from the crest of the foothill.

My experience reminded me of the problems one encounters when he does not have a proper perspective. What looks obvious from one point of view is altogether different when seen from another perspective. If you want to make valid judgments about things, it is necessary to have a proper perspective. Without a correct point of view, deciding what to do—and then attempting to do it—frequently leads to futility.

There can be no better place to begin a study of God than from the perspective that *he exists*. There are a number of reasons why this is an appropriate starting point.

One of the reasons to begin with the existence of God is that he is not very real to many of us who live in the twentieth century. As a matter of fact, contemporary society attempts to suppress discussion about God. Everybody knows that in polite society you don't talk about God or politics. Such discussions can only lead to arguments, so courteous people tend to avoid them.

With this kind of social pressure around us, it is important for Christians to remind themselves that God *really does* exist. God can have no reality for people who doubt his existence, or fail self-consciously to acknowledge his existence.

Another reason to look at the existence of God is that, without God, Christianity makes no sense. The Christian religion is based upon the assumption that there is a God in heaven. It's not just *any* god, either. The God of Christianity is a particular God, a God who reveals himself to us and clearly describes his character for us.

Historically, Protestants have started their thinking about religion by looking at the existence of God. Examine, for example, the writings of our Puritan forebears, or Scottish Presbyterians, or John Calvin, and you will find that all of them center on who God is. Each of these people not only acknowledged that God existed—they based all their thinking about religion on that foundation. These our forebears clearly believed that man exists for God's sake, and they insisted that the God who existed was their God. He was the God who, because he existed, benefited his people.

Twentieth-century Christians need the same vision that characterized Puritan New England and Calvin's Geneva. We need a sense of God's existence and a desire to love and serve him. Our society has pushed God far from us. Those of us who are in the Christian church must rediscover the glory of God and the reality of his existence. We must take note of this in every aspect of our life. God can never be a mere abstraction; he must be a God who makes a difference in our lives.

Those Who Deny the Existence of God

There are two types of people who deny that God exists. The first are those we call "atheists." These are people who say that belief in God is silly or unsophisticated. They are of the opinion that those who believe in God are throwbacks to some less-civilized era. Since the rise of modern science, atheists more and more use science alone to explain what happens in this world. They claim that they no longer need God to account for the unknown. They are confident that science will one day enable them to understand everything—nothing will be incomprehensible to them.

There is a much larger group who do not believe in God. We could call these people "practical atheists." They don't self-consciously deny the existence of God, but subconsciously they are doing exactly that. These people simply live as if God did not exist. If you followed them around, if you talked with them, if you examined their thought life, you would note that God doesn't play any role at all in their lives. About the only time they refer to God is when they use his name in profanity.

Sad to say, practical atheism can even infect the church. There are any number of Christians who lack a self-conscious realization that God exists. In fact, almost all Christians experience this phenomenon at one time or another. And when they do, they are thinking atheistically and are, for all practical purposes, atheists.

As Christians, we ought to move away from this kind of practical atheism. We need to be self-consciously aware of God's existence. In reality, we should move even beyond that. It's not enough to say, "Yes, I acknowledge in my thought life that God exists." We ought to be able to say that it makes a great difference to us. We shouldn't just say, as we work, that we recognize that God exists; rather, we should say, "I work in a certain way *because* God exists."

Arguments for the Existence of God

For years theologians have tried to demonstrate the existence of God. They call these demonstrations "theistic proofs." Some argue that, because people the world over have a concept of a Supreme Being, there must be some reality behind the idea.

11

If God *didn't* exist, people would not have any idea about him, and all of their reasoning would be false. Theologians call this the *ontological* proof for God's existence.

Another argument for the existence of God is based on the evidence in creation. The only possible explanation for the existence of creation, they reason, is that God made everything. Someone needed to start bringing all the world into being, and that First Cause of everything was God. People refer to this as the *cosmological* proof.

A third argument grows out of the idea of purpose or design. When we study anything, from the solar system to a microscopic cell, we see design and purpose. This can be possible only if there is some intelligent being who gives the elements of the universe purpose or design. The intelligent being is God, who first caused everything and gave it purpose. Those who use this line of argument employ the *teleological* proof for God's existence.

It is interesting to note that the Bible doesn't spend a whole lot of time proving that God exists. Note that Moses, as he writes in the early chapters of Genesis, doesn't argue that God exists; he simply *assumes* that he does. The Bible begins with the proper perspective: God does indeed exist. We too must begin with that perspective. This does not mean that proofs for God's existence are unimportant or irrelevant to us. Not at all. Indeed, they can help to confirm our belief in his existence.

Again, in Psalm 19 the psalmist assumes that God exists, but doesn't argue the point. He tells us that all the things in this world show us something about God: the heavens declare his glory, the firmament shows his handiwork. The Bible handles theistic proofs for the existence of God as confirmations of what we already believe.

In Psalm 139, the psalmist once again assumes God's existence. No matter where the writer goes, he can't escape from the awareness of God's existence. If he goes to the top of the highest point, God is there. If he makes his bed in Sheol, God is present. He is everywhere, and he reminds the psalmist of his existence. This is the manner in which the Bible argues about God's reality.

It doesn't attempt to prove it, but constantly assumes that he exists.

Everything in creation reminded the ancient Hebrews of God. They saw that all of life pointed to the truth that God existed. They went as far as to say that only a fool would deny the existence of God (see Psalm 14).

God and the Gods

Some Christians are confused when they look at the Old Testament. They find the Bible talking not only about the true God, but also about other gods. If there is only one God, then who are these others that the Scriptures mention?

We find a similar confusion in the twentieth century. There are those who say that there are many gods, who are invented by individuals to meet their individual needs. God, according to the skeptic, is something for people to fall back on when the going gets rough. For some he is like a warm puppy that, when they think about him, makes them feel confident.

The Bible claims that the various gods do not really exist, but are mere figments of people's imaginations. Nonexistent gods are contrasted sharply with the one who is real. Clearly portrayed in the Bible is the one only true and living God.

One thing is perfectly clear when we look at the Scriptures: The writers of the Bible have come to grips with the reality of God's existence. It's not something they merely speculate about. They recognize his being intellectually and experience it to the fullest extent in their lives.

The human authors of Scripture recognized the folly of attributing reality to other gods. They knew they were unreal—they couldn't, for instance, answer prayer. They recognized also the spiritual bankruptcy of those who called upon false gods. We need the same kind of awareness.

The Reality of God's Existence

The Bible makes it plain that God's existence is not imaginary, but is something that touches every aspect of our lives. It has a fundamental reality that the ancient Hebrew found impossible to deny.

You can see this in the way the Bible describes God in such clear and obvious terms. He is a God who has made known specifics about himself, some of which are essential while others are merely incidental. They are things that God has revealed to the writers of the Bible in order to transform their lives in various ways.

For example, Scripture throughout bears consistent witness to the *holiness* of God, who not only has never sinned but is utterly incapable of sinning. "Holy, holy, holy is the LORD Almighty; the whole earth is full of his glory" (Isaiah 6:3). Fallen man could never have conceived of holiness had the Scriptures not displayed it as an essential attribute of the God who is.

Acquiring the Proper Perspective

One of the purposes of this book is to help you to acquire the proper perspective. As you think about what the Bible says about the nature and character of God, you will begin to see things from his point of view. It is amazing how coming to understand the various aspects of God's being helps you to think about life from a godly perspective.

In this book we will look at the fact that only the God of the Bible is truly God; there is no other. This is sure to make a difference. With this knowledge you will be able to cut through the falsehoods of those who speak favorably of the benefits of the eastern mystery religions.

The fact that God makes himself known is dealt with in a later chapter. As we look at what God says about himself—that he is light, love and Spirit, for example—we should find ourselves better equipped to behave as God desires. Because God is light, Christians can resist the power of Satan, the prince of darkness. In the midst of the most trying circumstances of life, we can find comfort and confidence in the knowledge that God loves us and will never abandon us. Our neighbor may question how we can serve someone we cannot see, but *we* know that our God is a spirit and is always near—even when our neighbors mock us!

In the following chapters the power, wisdom and goodness of God will be examined. As you reflect on these attributes of God, these characteristics of his personality, you will find that your assurance that God does indeed exist will grow. You will also become increasingly aware that following and serving him is the right thing to do.

You can acquire the proper perspective on life, not only from studying a book like this that tells you what the Bible teaches about God, but also from observing his handiwork in creation. Some clear night go out and look into the sky. How amazing that the powerful God who made all these remote things also created you—and is ever close to you. This should help you join with the psalmist who saw the heavens as the handiwork of God and praised him for "your heavens, the work of your fingers, the moon and the stars, which you have set in place" (Psalm 8:3).

Responding to the Proper Perspective

One of the results of acknowledging that God exists is that it has an effect on the way we think. God becomes the central point of our thought processes. We seek to think God's thoughts after him, and in so doing our intellectual life is transformed.

We ought to see the effects of acknowledging God's existence in other ways as well. The recognition that God exists ought to enable us to love him. If he doesn't exist, we can't love him. But since he does exist, we must love him and serve him.

Our love for God is not like some adolescent fantasy. We can't make him exist by thinking it would be nice to love him— it's not like that at all. Rather, we love God *because* he exists. Because God is the kind of God he is, a God of love, we can love him. Not only *can* we love him—we *must* love him.

Because God is, we are enabled to set our affections upon him. Even though we cannot see him, still we can have confidence that our love for him is not foolish. When we know that God exists, we can have confidence in our love for him and his love for us.

God's existence should not call forth only our love; it ought also to call forth our service. The God of the Bible is one whom we can serve with joy and satisfaction. Service can take a multitude of forms, one of which is to *obey*. God tells us that, because he exists and is holy, we also are to be holy. We ought to be obedient, we ought to follow his law. This kind of behavior necessarily follows from the conviction that God really is. The Bible constantly assumes that God exists and makes demands upon all people to obey and serve him.

Everything in this world that reminds us that God exists should also remind us that we can and must love and serve him. If the heavens declare his glory and the firmament shows his handiwork, then these things ought also to call us to love and service. In Psalm 139 the psalmist talks about the body that God has so wondrously fashioned. If we are conscious of our bodies, we should equally be aware that the God who made them exists. We ought also to be conscious that we should love this God and serve him faithfully.

Review Questions

1. Define what is meant by the "proper perspective."
2. What point of view does the Bible take with regard to the existence of God?
3. Describe some of the proofs that have been used to show that God exists.
4. What are some of the characteristics of a practical atheist?
5. What has been the hallmark of the theology of protestant Christianity?

Discussion Questions

1. What type of person would be helped by an explanation of the proofs for God's existence?

2. How would you describe the proper perspective to a 13-year-old?
3. Describe a time when you behaved as a practical atheist. How would you correct such a viewpoint?
4. Describe a time when you dealt with an issue from the proper perspective. How can you cultivate this attitude toward life?
5. If the psalmist were writing Psalm 19 today, what figures of speech do you think he would use to convey the proper perspective?

There Is But One God

* God Alone!

Monotheism: "THE DOCTRINE OR BELIEF that there is but one God." So says Webster's dictionary.

For some of us, monotheism is a word that we learned in school when we studied world religions. Apart from that study, most western Europeans and Americans don't think about whether they are monotheists or not—our culture mostly assumes monotheism. When we use the word *god*, we are speaking of only one deity. But did you ever meet someone who wasn't a monotheist? Are there really people who live in modern, scientifically advanced, civilized cultures who are polytheists—who believe in more than one god? The two cases that follow should help you to judge for yourself.

The Changs are an interesting couple. They came separately to the United States from rural villages in the Orient as undergraduate students. They met at the university where they were both in medical school. They married and now practice medicine in their own thriving pediatric clinic. They also engage in all sorts of strange religious practices, among which are ceremonies designed to placate angry gods and honor departed ancestors. Surely they are not monotheists; yet they live in, and are a part of, our sophisticated technological culture.

The Jenisons are different—they don't practice *any* religion. A meal in their home is interesting: if some one spills the salt, he throws some over his shoulder; when they want something good to happen, they knock on wood; the parents constantly remind the children never to do anything that would dishonor the reputation of the family that their grandfather established in the community—after all, they wouldn't want to displease a departed loved one.

Two modern families, neither of which is monotheistic. In the first case, the Changs have kept their traditional notions about the gods of their ancestors and the need to appease the various deities whom they may have angered. The form of polytheism they practice in the United States is no different than what is seen frequently in many primitive societies.

In the second case, the Jenisons similarly show a disposition toward polytheism. Their little quirks are designed to placate the household deities. The superstitious behavior exhibited by the Changs and the Jenisons is similar to the polytheistic practices of people throughout history.

In the first chapter we examined practical atheism. The Chang and Jenison families may protest that, even though they do these things, they don't take them seriously. Nevertheless, they are examples of practical polytheism. Even though they do not follow the practice of polytheism as sincerely as did their forbears, they are nevertheless non-monotheists. Polytheism is a heresy that has tempted people in all ages of history.

It is no wonder that the Bible constantly emphasizes the theme that there is but one God. Scripture refers to other gods only to reveal their fraudulent character, taking pains to demonstrate that the other gods are altogether different from Yahweh God.

Yahweh Versus Non-Gods

One place where we can see the difference between the true God and non-gods or false gods is in 1 Kings 18, where we find the story of the encounter between Elijah and the prophets of Baal on Mount Carmel. The contrast between the true

God and non-gods is set in the context of a contest. The story is familiar to many of us, but perhaps looking at the details of the confrontation will help us to focus our attention on the distinctions.

In this passage, we see a striking disparity between the legitimacy of Yahweh and Baal's lack of authenticity. The prophets of Baal did everything imaginable to try to get their god to hear them and to answer their pleas. It is fairly clear, as we look at all the shenanigans they went through, that Baal was not going to acknowledge them. The story leaves us with only one reason for that: Baal simply doesn't exist. He is not really a god.

Elijah forced this issue by taunting the frustrated prophets. He asked whether Baal was out for a walk, or perhaps busy someplace else.

When the contest came to an end, Elijah once again demonstrated the power and authenticity of God. He called upon the name of God, but only after he had made it difficult for God to answer. After wetting down the altar and all the surrounding area, he simply called upon the name of God. There was no long, elaborate ritual. Immediately God answered with fire from heaven.

The only conclusion we can draw from the story is that Yahweh God exists, and Baal does not. Baal is not the true God; he is a false god, a nonexisting god.

Israel's History and the Non-Gods

The history of Israel is an account of a people continuously linked to the one true God. In contrast, other nations were followers of non-gods or false gods. But Israel's identification with the true God was not without compromise. From the beginning of her history, Israel was frequently vulnerable to temptations to add the worship of idols and other false gods to her religious life.

You may recall what happened when Jacob and his children tried to escape from Laban, who was pursuing them. When Laban caught up with them, he claimed to be looking for his stolen gods. We must assume they were used by Jacob's family. So the worship of false gods was something that often marked the children of Israel, even this early in her history (Genesis 31).

Later, while Moses was up in the mountain receiving the Ten Commandments from God, the Israelites were at the bottom making a false god. Remember—this was after God had demonstrated in such marvelous and miraculous terms that he alone was God. How could any Israelite doubt the superiority of Yahweh after the contest with the gods of Egypt?

Nevertheless, the Israelites built a false god, the golden calf, at the beginning of their journey to reestablish their nation in the land of promise. Was it gullibility on the part of the Israelites that caused them to do this? Aaron justified his actions on the basis of naïveté, stating that he had thrown the gold into the fire, and out came the calf. Even more amazing is the claim by the people that this calf was their *god*. How could this conceivably occur in ancient Israel, especially at this time? Had there not been enough dramatic demonstrations of the sole existence of the living God (Exodus 32)?

As has been pointed out, in Israel's history there was often an intermingling of the worship of the true God with the veneration of false gods. For example, as Joshua was preparing to lead Israel into the promised land, he declared to the people that he and his house were determined to follow the true God. He also reminded them that, on the other side of the river, their forbears had worshiped false gods (Joshua 24). Before the people entered the land of Canaan, which was a place of vile idolatry, they should determine whether they would worship Yahweh or the false gods of the nations.

The remainder of the Old Testament is a commentary on how inconsistently the people followed Joshua and his household. Israel's history is a continuing saga of the interplay between worshiping the true and living God and foolishly chasing after non-gods or false gods.

This may have been true even of David's family. What was it that Michal placed in the bed to trick the soldiers of her father, Saul, when they came looking for David? She placed an idol in the bed, and they thought it was David, who she alleged was sick. One can only assume the idol belonged to the household and was perhaps in use (1 Samuel 19).

This sin of following after false gods frequently plagued Israel. Their inability to recognize that gods other than Yahweh were non-gods was a continuing problem for the people.

Twentieth-century Christians are frequently baffled at the way the Old Testament people worshiped false gods. We profess not to know how they could possibly have been so unfaithful. We characterize these ancient people as naive and foolish. But we must be careful. We can't just condemn the folly of the Israelites, even though it is wide open to condemnation. We too must take the warnings of Scripture to heart. Like those ancient people, we too can fall into similar temptations.

The Power of False Gods

Some may find it difficult to understand the relationship between Yahweh and the false gods. If they are not real gods or if they don't exist, how come they seem to have supernatural power? This is a good question that should not be avoided.

One of the reasons for the confusion is that the Bible calls the false gods by the word *god*. We should not conclude from this that they are really gods. Rather, we must start with the premise that the Scriptures are built upon—*Yahweh* is God and there is none other.

People attribute the exercise of power to these false, non-existent gods. In fact, they are credited with supernatural acts. Nevertheless, they are not really gods. They are what the New Testament refers to as *angels, demons and powers* (Romans 8:38). They are devils or other forms of supernatural entities. They are not to be worshiped or adored in any way, but are to be treated as evil, as deceivers. They are instruments of their father, Satan. So we must distinguish between gods and beings who are able to engage in supernatural activities. The Bible uniformly attests to the uniqueness of Yahweh, while at the same time warning that there are other powers in the world.

These powers are always subservient to God, and are not his equal in any way. They are created by him, and they exist to fulfill his grand purposes. In a strange and mysterious way they do the bidding of Yahweh, the sovereign God of heaven and earth. In fact, even they acknowledge that the true God exists: "You believe that there is one God. Good! Even the demons believe that—and shudder" (James 2:19).

The relationship between all created supernatural beings (whether good or evil) and the true God is always the same. Unlike the false gods, these do exist, but they are clearly subservient to God. They are not real gods. If they purport to be such, they are lying and seeking to deceive. We should not be naive and assume that, because a being exercises power, it is a god. Neither should we assume that the forces of evil do not possess supernatural powers. What we must remember is that the one true God rules over all. He and he alone is God: there is none like him.

Affirming the One True God

In Deuteronomy 4:35, Moses reflected on all the things that had happened to the children of Israel, pointing out that these events transpired in order to demonstrate that there was one God. The people of Israel were to teach their children and their grandchildren about the various events that had transpired, so that they might know that there is one God only, Yahweh God.

David followed the lead of Moses. In the Psalms he constantly reminds us that there is only one God. Notice in Psalms 83 and 86 that David confirms that there is no god like the true God. It is a recurring theme of his.

You will note also that the first two commandments underscore the exclusivity of God. In fact, the whole of the Ten Commandments is predicated on this concept. The charter of the Israelite nation was founded on the basis of the fact that there is one God. And we in the twentieth-century church also have to have this as our fundamental starting point.

As we look at the Old Testament, we can conclude that there is only one dominant theme: *There is one God only.* The glorious refrain is repeated chapter after chapter, page after page, throughout.

Yet the Bible repeatedly complains that the people of the Old Testament constantly forgot there was only one God. This record is also useful as a reminder to us: *There is only one God.* Unlike the forgetful ancients, we twentieth-century moderns must take serious account of the Bible's repeated warnings.

False Gods of Today

Frequently we are just as adept as the people of the Old Testament era at inventing false gods. We, like they, constantly need to be warned to keep ourselves from idols and to be reminded that there is only one true God.

We are a little more sophisticated about the way in which we invent false gods. Very few Americans have idols in a corner of the living room. That sort of behavior would be odd, and unheard of from those who call themselves Christians. Nevertheless, we do have ways in which we invent non-gods and then seek to serve and follow them.

Think, for example, of the kind of superstitions that surround us. How many of us, when things are going well, will use words like "Knock on wood"? How many people have a lucky charm or rabbit's foot that they carry around to assure good luck? People not only carry these around out of tradition, but they expect that they will do them some good. People can be genuinely frustrated at the loss of some kind of a charm. They won't undertake certain activities unless they have their lucky piece with them.

The Cause of Idolatry

We are constantly attributing the power of God to some foolish non-divine entity. As soon as we ascribe the power of God to anything other than God, we are involved in the same

25

type of senseless idolatry that characterized the Israelites. We too are taking non-gods as gods and seeking to follow them.

Not only do we have these simple and unsophisticated techniques for manufacturing false gods, but we have more cultivated and complex ones as well. Technology has become one of the clearest and most obvious types of false gods in the twentieth century. We attribute to science abilities that should be ascribed to God alone.

We seem to believe that technological advances can really alleviate all of our problems. We imagine they can answer all the questions that confront mankind. We constantly honor technology by assuming that it will overcome any and all of life's obstacles.

Examples of our unbounded confidence in technology cover a wide range of issues. Some people go so far as to want their bodies frozen, and then thawed out when a cure for what is about to kill them has been discovered. They actually believe that applied science can eventually keep them from death.

Others contend that, with the correct blend of education and other services, we can eliminate crime. There are many well-meaning people who think that better delivery systems for social services can circumvent problems that are caused by sin. In fact, they believe there is no such thing as sin—there is only ignorance and a negative environment.

This unjustified trust in the power of technology leads people to do more than seek solutions to their problems. They actually believe that confidence in the industrial arts is all that is necessary for a satisfying life. Technology becomes their god.

But honoring technology is simply a way of commending ourselves. Having replaced God with our own creations, we worship and adore the imaginations and thoughts of our evil hearts. This is the core of idolatry and the worship of all false gods. It is an attempt by the creature to make himself equal to God. This was what Adam and Eve did in the Garden of Eden, and many today are continuing to follow their sinful pattern.

It is clear that our sophisticated twentieth-century society is not immune to temptations to manufacture false gods for ourselves. What *has* changed is the way in which we go about it. Perhaps we are not as naive as the ancient Israelites, but we are just as inclined to fall into the same pattern of idolatry. The only difference is our degree of proficiency and the use of more technological devices to accomplish these things.

The Folly of False Gods

Perhaps one of the best illustrations of the folly of making false gods is portrayed by the prophet Isaiah (Isaiah 44). He talks about people who cut down a tree to form a god, and then with the leftover wood heat a meal for themselves. Ridiculous, we say. But it is no more preposterous to make gods out of wood than it is to form them out of our vain imaginations.

In the New Testament we find a similar condemnation of the worship of false gods. Perhaps the most definitive statement is that of Paul in his Corinthian correspondence. In 1 Corinthians 8:4–6 he reminds us that there *are* no other gods. There is one God only, the Father of our Lord Jesus Christ.

Belief in one God is important. This conviction should do more than keep us from making and worshiping false gods. When we are convinced there is only one God, we must acknowledge him openly.

Acknowledging the One True God

This acknowledgment can come in the midst of worship. Honoring God as the one and only true God is a characteristic theme of the Psalms. The psalmist declares, "For great is the LORD and most worthy of praise; he is to be feared above all gods. For all the gods of the nations are idols, but the LORD made the heavens. Splendor and majesty are before him; strength and glory are in his sanctuary" (Psalm 96:4–6). Then the psalmist proceeds to list various ascriptions of praise that should be made to God. He calls upon the people to "worship the Lord in the splendor of his holiness; tremble before him, all the earth" (verse 9).

If there is only one God, then worshiping him is mandatory. Do you join with your fellow believers, Sunday after Sunday, with the expectation that the heavens will rejoice, the earth will be glad, the sea and everything in it will resound, the fields and everything in them will be jubilant and the trees will sing for joy because of the one true God (Psalm 96:11, 12)? Being in the presence of the only God week in and week out should cause more excitement than watching the World Series! Do you respond to your conviction that there is only one God as the psalmist prescribes?

If there is only one God, we shouldn't be confused by competing loyalties. God must come before our job, our hobbies, and even our families.

We are to love him with all our heart. And then we can serve him with all that is in us.

Review Questions

1. What are some examples of polytheism today?
2. How did Elijah demonstrate that there is only one God?
3. How does the Bible describe gods other than Yahweh?
4. What is the source of idolatry?
5. What is an appropriate way to acknowledge that there is only one God?

Discussion Questions

1. How can you avoid falling prey to idolatry?
2. What reasons do you think the Israelites would have given to justify making the golden calf? What are some contemporary parallels?
3. What are some ways that Christians today do the same thing the Israelites did with regard to false gods?
4. How can one have a healthy appreciation of modern technological developments without attributing godlike qualities to them?

5. Is idolatry a danger in your life? If so, what are you doing to avoid the danger? If not, how have you kept yourself from it?

God Makes
Himself Known

MARY AND SAM have been married for 12 years. They have three fine youngsters, and are thought well of by their neighbors; but the success of their marriage is a cause of wonder among some of their friends. You see, Mary and Sam never saw one another until two days before they were married.

They did know all about one another, however. In fact, people who don't know them frequently assume they were childhood sweethearts. They laugh about things that happened to each other as children, joke about idiosyncrasies of their parents, and they are familiar with each other's families. It has been this way as long as anyone can remember.

How could two people who met one another only two days before their wedding know so much about each other? At age 11, Mary and Sam became pen pals. Even though they never met, they shared all their childhood experiences. As they grew older, their relationship changed into something much more complex. After years of writing to one another, they decided they knew each other well enough to get married.

You see, each one took the initiative in making himself or herself known, and their knowledge of one another plays a large part in their happy marriage. Even before they met, they knew each other well. Sam and Mary obviously love one another and live to serve one another.

If we are going to love and serve God, it will be necessary

for us to know something about him. This should not seem unusual. What *is* striking though, is that God takes the prime role in making himself known. For it would be impossible for us to appreciate God if he did not take the lead in revealing himself.

If we wanted to know something about someone, perhaps the first thing we would do would be to ask for a picture. But God does not function in this manner—this is not how he chooses to disclose his person and attributes. He gives us no photo; in fact, he tells us he doesn't want us to have visual images of him.

The reason for this: God is a *spirit*. Even young children, as they memorize a child's catechism, can realize that God is a spirit and doesn't have a body as men do; and so they can understand why he doesn't reveal himself by means of a picture. This makes God different from all the false gods around us.

Revelation in Creation

One of the ways in which God reveals himself is through the things he has created. David, in Psalm 19, explains how God reveals himself in the world he made and governs:

> The heavens declare the glory of God; the skies proclaim the work of his hands. Day after day they pour forth speech; night after night they display knowledge. There is no speech or language where their voice is not heard. Their voice goes out into all the earth, their words to the ends of the world. In the heavens he has pitched a tent for the sun, which is like a bridegroom coming forth from his pavilion, like a champion rejoicing to run his course. It rises at one end of the heavens and makes its circuit to the other; nothing is hidden from its heat (Psalm 19:1–6).

The fact that God makes himself known by means of his created works is not the message only of this psalm—it is repeated regularly in the Scriptures. Here the psalmist is engaging in praise and worship because of what he knows about God on the basis of his handiwork. That should make good sense to us; we can learn much about people when we examine the things they make.

I frequently find myself doing this without much self-conscious thought. If I were to examine a set of bookcases you had made, I could tell whether you are careful or not. By looking at the joints I would know whether you are skilled, or just a novice. I would know whether you strive for excellence when I stroked the finish. If it was rough with uneven sanding and brush marks, I would know that you are satisfied with something far short of perfection.

Or perhaps I would examine a dress you had made. Your skill or lack of it would be obvious from the way in which the sleeves fit into the body of the dress. If the hem was straight, the zipper smooth and the pattern matched, I could be sure you were capable, patient and careful in handling details.

The same is also true of God. We come to realize many things about him as we investigate the things he has made.

Sinful Response to Revelation

Although the revelation of God in this world is clear, people frequently misinterpret it. The Bible tells us that, on the basis of what God has made, we can discern clear and obvious aspects of his character. There is no confusion in the created world itself; it shows us *God*. Any impediment to understanding resides exclusively with people.

Men and women refuse to acknowledge that the created universe reveals God's attributes. This self-deception is caused by mankind's sin.

> The wrath of God is being revealed from heaven against all the godlessness and wickedness of men who suppress the truth by their wickedness, since what may be known about God is plain to them, because God has made it plain to them. For since the creation of the world God's invisible qualities—his eternal power and divine nature—have been clearly seen, being understood from what has been made, so that men are without excuse (Romans 1:18–20).

In this passage Paul tells us that, when we observe what God has made, certain of his features—including his invisible qualities, his eternal power and divine nature—ought to be apparent to all of us. None is without excuse; when we look at the world, we ought to recognize and acknowledge everything they disclose about God.

Jesus provided a good example of this in the Sermon on the Mount (Matthew 6:25–34). He reminded his listeners that God cares even for the birds and the lilies of the field. How foolish it is, then, for us to worry! If God takes care of the animals, won't he care for his redeemed people? When we examine creation, we ought to see that God is glorious. The animal kingdom, the flowers of the field and the heavenly bodies—all display for us something of his invisible qualities, even his eternal Godhead. He intended for us to view his creation in this way and wants us to see him in the midst of his handiwork.

We find evidence of what God is like, not only in the birds and flowers and those things we commonly call nature, but also in the crown of creation, man. As we reflect on how our bodies are made and how they function, we should be conscious of God's power and wisdom. David, in Psalm 139:14, tells us that the human body is a marvelous thing; we are "fearfully and wonderfully made."

The marvel of the human body reveals aspects of God's wisdom. The structure of the body, the intricacy of the knee, the endurance of the heart—all show that God is wise.

Modern science has tried for years to duplicate ordinary occurrences in God's creation. For example, it has attempted to *create* life. Initiating new life has been an integral part of God's world since the beginning. The ability to establish life reminds us of God's uniqueness. No one has been able to copy whatever it was that God did to institute different forms of life, from the simplest to the most complex.

Because some of these things are so common in nature, we excuse our failure to see God's hand in them. But the fact that they are common is not the source of the problem. The issue is that mankind refuses to see God in the things he has created.

This is the point the apostle Paul makes in the early chapters of his letter to the Romans.

In fact, Paul tells us that sinful people take the obvious truths derived from the created universe, twist them, and hold them down so that they no longer point to their Creator. Instead of worshiping God, unbelievers abuse natural revelation and seek to honor the creature. They pervert the teaching of natural revelation so they can justify and excuse themselves. This allows them to worship the gods they choose rather than the God of creation. The irony of what Paul says is striking.

What the sinner does is to take things that are obvious to him and turn them in a different direction. God has made his world so that it points to himself as Creator, yet sinful people refuse to recognize God as such. In fact, they twist things around so that they worship, not the God who has created, but the creation itself.

A Map in a Mirror

Suppose you have bought a map, with the expectation that it will guide you to a certain place. It's a snap—all you have to do is follow the map, and there you are. Now, if you had done with your map what the foolish and sinful people described above have done with creation and its Creator, you would never have reached your destination. It would have been as though you had read your map held up to a mirror: left would have been right and right would have been left; east would have been west, and vice versa.

Yet that is how unbelievers handle God's revelation of himself in the world. They ignore the created things that point to God, and so travel in the wrong direction. Instead of worshiping the Creator, they end up worshiping the creature. Not seeing this as a serious matter, they naively imagine that all is well and that they are headed in the right direction.

If you have young children, you may have observed a similar phenomenon. You tell the kids to do something, and they do the opposite. You say to your child, "Didn't I tell you not to play with the pen?" The child will look at you in all innocence and say, "But I didn't play with the pen; I was going to write a letter to Grandma." Perhaps unwittingly, the child has disobeyed you, and you are displeased. Childishly naive, he too will not understand that punishment may be in the offing.

No matter how explicit your instructions, children can manage to distort them in such a way as to satisfy themselves that they have obeyed you. Grown-ups do much the same thing with God's self-revelation through creation; but their offense is greater because theirs is the sin of ignoring or openly rejecting the revelation.

Revelation in Word

We are often just like our children. We take the revelation of God in the world and pervert it. God's creation is sufficient for us to recognize that he is God. Our problem is that we just haven't looked at it properly. The marvel is that God not only gave us the world that points us to him, his Word also directs us to him. It also reveals that we handle the creation in a perverse way.

We could go back to Psalm 19 and see how it tells us not only about God's creation, but also about his Word. See, for example, how the psalmist treats the law of the Lord: it guides us to God. Psalm 119 also offers us a ready entry into the storehouse of blessings provided by the Word for our growth. This longest chapter of the Bible is a song in praise of God for his Word. And so we see that he not only reveals himself in general ways through the world, but also specifically through his Word.

The usefulness of God's Word in helping us to understand who he is was evident from the time of Adam and Eve in the garden. God not only put them in the midst of the world, he also came and spoke to them personally. They came to know what God wanted and who God was.

He not only made himself known as he spoke to people, he also kept a record of it. That is what we have in Scripture—a record of God's dealings with man. We have a record of what he said to individuals. We have a record of what he did in dealing with the nations. We even have a record of some of his reflections on his dealings with humanity.

For example, God spelled out to Moses how the Israelites should live. In giving the law, God revealed something about himself. He showed that he is a holy God who is perfectly righteous. The entire sacrificial system echoes with evidence of God's mercy and compassion. The children of Israel were to keep themselves from idols because God is a jealous God.

The entire book of Exodus opens up the character of God as it sets forth his laws and records his actions. For example, in the choosing of Israel we find confirmation of God's grace. In the destruction of his enemies we see an affirmation of his justice and his power.

The Role of the Word

The Scriptures help us not only to know something about God, but also to understand all the other aspects of his revelation. The Bible can be compared to my eyeglasses. They enable me to bring objects into focus so they are no longer distorted. They help me to clear up a muddled field of vision. The Bible, like my glasses, can help me to see God as he is displayed in the creation—without distortion.

The very fact that God makes himself known tells us something about him. It tells us that he is gracious; he doesn't want us to be ignorant of who he is. It also tells us something about his holiness; he does not want us to have false or confused ideas about his character and nature. The fact that God has given us the Scriptures also tells us that God wants to communicate with us. He has made us to have fellowship with him, and he takes steps to see that this is possible.

In summary, then, we can see that God reveals himself in the things he has made. The world around us shows us something about God. We also know that God reveals himself in his Word, the Bible. This special or particular revelation helps us to understand the general revelation in creation. Not only does God reveal himself in the world and through his Word, but he also reveals himself through his Son. Hebrews 1 tells us that in these last days that's the way in which God has come to reveal himself. The revelation that Jesus Christ brings is the apex of God's self-revelation.

Responding to Revelation

As God's people, we are obligated to utilize the revelation God has given us. We must not neglect, ignore or despise God's self-revelation

This means that spring days are not to be taken up exclusively with thoughts of baseball. Rather, we should be reflecting on the resurgence of nature, and how it shows us God's power. We ought to be reminded that God brings the sunshine and the rain. We should take comfort in the fact that God consistently brings springtime and harvest, and that he will faithfully care for us with unfailing affection.

We have been prodded, more times than we care to recall, to study our Bibles. The reason for the constant reminders is that we need to study God's written communication to us. There is no better way to come to know God than to immerse ourselves in his Word.

As we handle properly the totality of God's revelation of himself, we are showing our love. The loving study of his self-revelation causes our love for him to grow.

The study of God's revelation of himself is also an exercise in serving him. Those who serve God in this way are equipped to serve more effectively as they engage in further works of service. As we serve God, we come to know him better.

The Christian who wants to love and serve God can find no better place to begin than with God's revelation of himself.

Review Questions

1. Why does God reveal himself?

2. What two types of revelation do we have from God?
3. How do different people respond to God's revelation?
4. What does the unbeliever do with God's revelation of himself in creation?
5. What role does word revelation play in understanding revelation in creation?

Discussion Questions

1. Make a list of the characteristics of God that are evident in creation.
2. Is God's revelation of himself in creation sufficient? Why or why not?
3. What steps can you take to benefit from God's revelation of himself in creation and in the Word?
4. What would mankind be like if God had not made himself known in creation? in word? in both?
5. How can you show God you appreciate his revelation of himself in creation, in the Word?

God Became Man

A NUMBER OF YEARS AGO, during a medical emergency in our home, my family and I experienced an extraordinary outpouring of kindness and thoughtfulness from Christian friends. My wife was confined to bed for a few months because of an illness. While she was bedridden, members of our church helped us in a variety of ways. They brought in meals, helped clean the house, and undertook innumerable other little jobs that my wife was unable to do.

Not only did they take care of the jobs around the house, they also visited regularly with my wife. She enjoyed talking with Christian friends during the long hours she had to spend in bed. They often prayed for her recovery, and for our strength to be able to bear up during this difficult time in our lives.

I couldn't think of ways to thank them, let alone repay them for all the wonderful, thoughtful and kind ways in which they treated us. Even now, several years later, I remember how marvelous those children of God were in dealing with us. I am still amazed and grateful.

A Personal God

Astonished though I am to have been a recipient of such kindness, it pales in comparison to what God has done for us. No matter what wonderful things may happen to us, they cannot compare to what God has done in making himself known. For God became man, and in doing so made himself known more fully to us than would have been possible in any other way.

In the previous chapter, we examined other ways in which God reveals himself. We looked first at how God reveals himself in the world he has made. We also saw how God makes himself known in the creation of man. We surveyed the character of man, and how the fact that we are made in God's image tells us something about the personality of God. We noted such things as the moral character of man and God, as well as the communication skills of each.

A second way in which God reveals himself is in his talking to man. This is especially the case in the Word of God, the Bible. We paid some attention to the acts of God that are recorded in Scripture, and tried to discover what they have to tell us about the nature and character of God.

Christ, the Word in Flesh

We finally arrived at the point at which God made himself known in the second person of the Trinity—that is, through Jesus Christ. How is it that God revealed himself through his Son? Perhaps the best place to begin is with the first chapter of John's Gospel.

> In the beginning was the Word, and the Word was with God, and the Word was God. He was with God in the beginning. Through him all things were made; without him nothing was made that has been made. In him was life, and that life was the light of men. The light shines in the darkness, but the darkness has not understood it....He was in the world, and though the world was made through him, the world did not recognize him. He came to that which was his own, but his own did not receive him. Yet to all who received him, to those who believed in his name, he gave the right to become children of God—children born not of natural descent, nor of human decision or a husband's will, but born of God. The Word became flesh and made his dwelling among us. We

have seen his glory, the glory of the One and Only, who came from the Father, full of grace and truth (John 1:1–5, 10–14).

Christ Reveals the Father

The above passage, in declaring that Jesus (who is the Son of God) became man, tells us something about God. He is gracious and kind, because he sent his Son to show men what the Father is like. He did not need to do this, but he did it— entirely for our good. Here we get an insight into the personality and character of God as we learn of his glory, grace and truth. And when we look at Jesus, we see these same characteristics.

The passage also teaches about God's eternality. Note the similarity with the first chapter of Genesis. In both passages, the writer takes on the proper perspective, assuming that God is present for all time. God is always there: he didn't have a beginning.

The incarnation reveals something of the nature of God: he took upon himself human flesh! This in itself demonstrates clearly the grace of God, for he who is the Maker took upon himself the form of the creature. In this one aspect of Jesus' humiliation, we see God as kind and gracious.

God Never Changes

The fact that God became man raises some questions in people's minds. Did God stop being God when he became man? Is Jesus no longer God? Some people appeal to Philippians 2:6, 7 to argue that Jesus ceased to be God when he became man.

Perhaps the best way to resolve these issues is to say that Jesus added to himself human form, with all the characteristics of man except sin. As the Shorter Catechism reminds us, Jesus, "being the eternal Son of God, became man and so was and continues to be God and man in two distinct natures and one person forever."

As you proceed with the remaining chapters of this book, you will note that all the characteristics of God that we will be studying are clearly seen in the person and work of Jesus. He shows us that God is light, for the Bible says that Jesus is the light of the world. And it is impossible to understand the Christian teaching that God is love apart from the work of Christ the Savior.

The Bible teaches that God is holy, and that he shows his holiness in his completely holy and perfect Son.

Even a small child can understand something of the goodness of God, when he sees how Jesus willingly laid down his life for his people. It is in Jesus that all of God's people are confronted with the overwhelming goodness of the Father who sent him to earth to redeem his people.

Perhaps it is on Easter, more than on any other day, that Christians recognize the power of God. He showed us his might by raising from the dead the Lord Jesus Christ. In his power he conquered our greatest enemy, death itself.

When we think about the plan of salvation—how a holy and righteous God can redeem unholy and unrighteous people—we are struck by the marvel of God's wisdom. It is only as we see what the faithful Son of the Father did—in bearing the punishment that our sins deserve so that the Father in heaven can be just and the justifier of his people—that we discern the wisdom of God. That is why the Bible can talk about wisdom personified, and we see it so in the person of the Savior.

We can love and serve God only as we come to understand, appreciate and claim for ourselves the marvelous work that Jesus has accomplished for his people. We must remember that Jesus did not come merely to show us what the Father in heaven is like; he came to do the will of his Father in order to accomplish the salvation of his people. That is why the apostle Paul can remind the people of the faithful saying, "Christ Jesus came into the world to save sinners" (1 Timothy 1:15).

In John 14:9–12 we find out more about God's character:

Jesus answered: "Don't you know me, Philip, even after I have been among you such a long time? Anyone who has seen me has seen the Father. How can you say, 'Show us the Father'? Don't you believe that I am in the Father, and that the Father is in me? The words I say to you are not just my own. Rather, it is the Father, living in me, who is doing his work. Believe in me when I say that I am in the Father and the Father is in me; or at least believe on the evidence of the miracles themselves. I tell you the truth, anyone who has faith in me will do what I have been doing."

Jesus was saying to Philip—and to all of us—that in his actions, statements and personality he is showing us who God is. We can know some important things about the nature of God, and to know more about Jesus Christ is to know more about the Father.

But what about us who have never seen Jesus? Do we have the same information Philip did? Although Jesus is no longer on earth, we have a trustworthy record of who he is. So the Word of God, the Bible, becomes important for us. It is our access to information about who Jesus is—and hence who God really is.

But God did not stop with the Son in making himself known. (Any one of the ways in which God has revealed himself would be sufficient to hold everyone accountable for knowing and acknowledging him. He has given all of these because he is a kind and gracious God.) He also sent the Holy Spirit, who works in us to enable us to understand and incorporate in our lives everything we have learned about God, through whichever of the agencies he has graciously used.

The Counsel of the Holy Spirit

But the Counselor, the Holy Spirit, whom the Father will send in my name, will teach you all things and will remind you of everything I have said to you (John 14:26).

The Spirit of God comes and teaches us everything that Jesus has said and done. The Spirit takes all the information we have and enables us to make it ours, so that we can love and serve God.

> Because I have said these things, you are filled with grief. But I tell you the truth: It is for your good that I am going away. Unless I go away, the Counselor will not come to you; but if I go, I will send him to you. When he comes, he will convict the world of guilt in regard to sin and righteousness and judgment: in regard to sin, because men do not believe in me; in regard to righteousness, because I am going to the Father, where you can see me no longer; and in regard to judgment, because the prince of this world now stands condemned. I have much more to say to you, more than you can now bear. But when he, the Spirit of truth, comes, he will guide you into all truth. He will not speak on his own; he will speak only what he hears, and he will tell you what is yet to come. He will bring glory to me by taking from what is mine and making it known to you. All that belongs to the Father is mine. That is why I said the Spirit will take from what is mine and make it known to you (John 16:6–15).

When Jesus left the disciples, the Holy Spirit enabled people to understand what it is that Jesus taught.

In Romans 8, Paul teaches that the Holy Spirit does something similar for us:

> Those who live according to the sinful nature have their minds set on what that nature desires; but those who live in accordance with the Spirit have their minds set on what the Spirit desires. The mind of sinful man is death, but the mind controlled by the Spirit is life and peace; the sinful mind is hostile to God. It does not submit to God's law, nor can it do so. Those controlled by the sinful nature cannot please God. You, however, are controlled not by the sinful nature but by the Spirit, if the Spirit of God lives in you. And if anyone does not have the Spirit of Christ, he does not belong to Christ. But if Christ is in you, your body is dead because of sin, yet your spirit is alive because of righteousness (5–10).

The variety of ways in which God makes himself known can be likened to a Christmas feast. After the appetizer, we have all probably had enough to eat. But there is something more, and still more after that. By the time we get to the main course, we are completely stuffed. And on top of that, there is of course dessert. So it is with the ways in which God reveals himself.

Denying God's Revelation

If it is the case that God makes himself known in the Bible, in creation and in Jesus, and he does so clearly, why is it that so many of us miss this revelation? Why do so few of us take advantage of what God gives to us? He takes the initiative in such a direct way, and still many refuse to acknowledge him.

Perhaps we miss God's revelation for the same reasons that we miss other things. Frequently when I go to look for something, I can't find it. I keep searching; finally (and fortunately!) my wife comes along and points out where it is. All of us have had similar experiences.

This illustrates why we miss God's revelation. We are looking at things, but we are unable to separate out what is significant from what is irrelevant. The unbelieving world is surely like this. All of God's revelation is there for them to see, but they just avoid recognizing and acknowledging it.

A False View of Revelation

Christians also will frequently miss what God is showing them, because they will look at the wrong things. They fail to pay attention to what is crucial—namely, those things that point us to God. Instead, they look at the world as if it were their own, and not God's.

I notice that I look at the Bible from a professional point of view. That is, the Bible gives me answers to questions that other people have asked. Or I look into the Bible to see what it is that ought to be taught to someone else. All of us can miss God's revelation of himself if we look at the wrong things, or look at his revelation without expecting to see what God has to say about himself.

Failure to Listen to God

People also miss what God is saying to them because they don't pay attention to him. They focus on something else. For example, I may sit down to talk with my wife, but there is a magazine beside me. My eyes may note an interesting picture or headline in the magazine. I don't resist reading the headline or the caption under the picture; in fact, I often begin reading articles in the magazine. I may be listening to my wife ever so slightly, but what I'm really doing is reading the magazine. I get in and out of the conversation. She will tell me something, and it won't register. Later, someone will tell me the very same thing, and I will repeat it to my wife. Then she gently reminds me that she told me about the incident earlier during our conversation.

The same thing can happen as we look at the world around us. We know that God is telling us something about himself, but we don't pay very close attention; so the point doesn't register with us. The sun comes up and we don't recognize that the Lord is telling us that this is another of his good gifts to the children of men. We read the Bible or listen to a sermon, but our minds wander. We are more concerned and interested in something else, even when God's Word to us about himself is before us.

There are also things that we just simply don't want to learn, because they make us uncomfortable. We don't like to be confronted with our sin in contrast to God's righteousness. Therefore we just avoid absorbing those things that God tells us about his purity. Or we may acknowledge them one time, and fail to remember them again.

We must be careful that we don't attribute our failure to comprehend God's revelation to a fault in communication. The information is sufficient and clear. It is our perception, or refusal to perceive, that is the cause of our failure to comprehend. We have perversely chosen, in one way or another, to avoid understanding what it is that God has made known about himself.

True Knowledge of God

We can make a distinction between knowing something about God's revelation of himself and knowing God himself. Many of us can give a clear answer to the question of who God is. For example, you may have memorized the definition in the answer to Question 4 of the Shorter Catechism: "God is a Spirit, infinite, eternal, and unchangeable in his being, wisdom, power, holiness, justice, goodness and truth." While knowing this answer may indicate that you know something about God's revelation, it doesn't guarantee that you know God himself.

Just because we can define or explain who God is does not mean that we know who God is. We can know about God without knowing who God is; the Bible is very clear about this. The biblical word for *know* involves more than simple cognition or having facts. Perhaps the best way to illustrate this is by recognizing that the Bible uses the word *know* to describe the most intimate of human encounters—namely, sexual intercourse. Knowledge is not just the storing up of facts, or checking off criteria for definitions; it involves close relationships. We know God when we have that kind of association with him.

Criteria for Knowing

If you were going to appear in court and were required to demonstrate to the judge that you knew someone, what sort of things would you use to convince the judge? Would you describe incidents in the individual's life, and perhaps try to draw conclusions about his character, based on your experience with him? Would you describe the sort of language he uses, or cite some names that people use for him? Would you tell the judge how much time you spend together or how you communicate with one another? Perhaps you would relate some ways in which the person helped you, or describe things that you have in common. Would you describe his physical appearance or his habits?

Note that you would not necessarily have to be articulate about the person. Rather, the things that would probably count would be those experiential things that you had in common with him. Well, in somewhat the same way, might it be that you could convince a judge that you know God?

For a number of years, I worked for a publishing company that sent out catalogs, samples, letters and brochures so that people would know what we produced. Frequently I met people who had received all of this material, but were surprised when I told them about something we manufactured. Receiving information is not the same as knowing something.

Knowing Through Relationship

Another way in which we can learn more about someone is by telling another person about him. I first experienced this when I went to a parent-teacher conference, and the teacher asked me some questions about my child. As I described my daughter to the teacher, there were other characteristics of hers that became clear in my mind. The same can be true of knowing God. If we try to tell others about him, not only does our understanding become clearer, but we also know him in a more experiential fashion

We can also understand God's revelation of himself to us better if we will tinker with it. I don't mean to *change* it, but to manipulate and work with it. I can remember the first time I got a pocket calculator. I read the little book that told me all the things that the device would do. But I was not very well acquainted with its attributes until I tinkered with it for awhile. That is how I really found out all the things it would do, and all the ways to do them. I'm sure you have had similar experiences. The same is true of God's self-revelation. Until we work with it, we will not really understand it.

Review Questions

1. How is Jesus the Word of God?

50

2. What is the role of the Holy Spirit?
3. How does the unbelieving world miss God's revelation?
4. How do Christians miss God's revelation?
5. What is true knowledge of God?

Discussion Questions

1. How would you explain the incarnation to a person who thinks that God is impersonal?
2. Explain the difference between the Spirit's role in the world and in the church.
3. Why is it important for the Christian to live under the control of the Holy Spirit?
4. Contrast the ability of the Christian to understand revelation with the inability of the unbeliever.
5. How would you direct a fellow Christian who is seeking to know God better?

God Is Spirit

SOME THINGS ARE EASY TO DESCRIBE—like your house, for example. You can tell someone how many rooms your house has, and describe the layout of the floor plan. You can picture with words the decorations in the house, and detailing the furnishings would give you no difficulty.

Why is it so easy to describe your house? One reason is that you have experienced your house with your senses of sight and touch. You are familiar with the odors and sounds of your home—so familiar, in fact, that if something is out of the ordinary, you almost immediately sense it. Your senses help you to apprehend—and then explain more fully—what your house is like.

In contrast, when we try to describe God as spirit, we run into difficulty. Because God is a spirit, we often falter when we try to explain what he is like. Frequently we are forced to use negative terms exclusively to describe God's spirituality. We have difficulty saying exactly what spirit is—we can only say what spirit is not. We lack the vocabulary to discuss spirit readily; it's not a part of our ordinary experience.

One of the few direct statements in the Bible about God's nature is "God is spirit" in John 4:24. Because the Bible makes such an unequivocal declaration about God's character, we must pay close attention to what it tells us. This important passage tells us who we are to worship, and one determining element in our worship is God's spirituality. Therefore we need to understand what the Bible means when it says that God is a spirit.

Spirit, One Without a Body

For some, the best place to look for a description of God as spirit is in the Westminster Confession of Faith or the Shorter Catechism. The Confession of Faith tells us that God is "a most pure spirit, invisible, without body, parts, or passions" (WCF, 2.1). The Shorter Catechism states that "God is a Spirit, infinite, eternal, and unchangeable" (Q. 9).

Some of us aren't helped a great deal by these statements; for us there is help in the directness of the children's *First Catechism*, which tells us that "God is a Spirit and has no body as we do." In trying to understand that God is a spirit, perhaps this is the best place to begin. Basically, a spirit is a person without a body.

When we realize that God is a spirit, we can understand a number of other things the Bible teaches.

Characteristics of God's Spirituality

One of the things we must realize is that, because God does not have a body, he is invisible. We cannot see, touch, taste or smell him—he is not apprehended by our senses. So if we claim that God can be seen with the eyes, we are making a false statement about God. God's spirituality is reflected in the second commandment. Since God is noncorporeal, it is illegitimate to make any image, picture or likeness of him.

Some may wonder how the Bible can talk about God as having hands, feet, eyes, ears, nose and mouth. You should know that these expressions are only ways to help us to understand how God acts. Because he is a spirit, he does not actually have these parts; but because we associate the functions of these bodily parts with the parts themselves, God accommodates his description of himself to our limited understanding, and uses such language. We need to realize, however, that God really does hear, see and feel. We don't know what God as pure spirit uses to hear, but whatever it is, our ears approximate it—we might say that our hearing with the ears of our bodies is a functional equivalent of whatever God uses. We need to remember that God is the original, we are the image bearer.

God is a pure spirit. This means that he is not like us, part body and part non-body; he is only spirit. Again, this probably raises a question as we try to understand what God is like. We can acknowledge that there is a part of us that is not material, such as the part of us that feels sad. But we have difficulty thinking that someone could exist who had no part of himself that was not immaterial.

Since God has no body, it is possible for him to show himself in many different forms. The Old Testament appearances of God are varied; for instance, he can resemble a cloud, a pillar of fire, or a burning bush. None of these appearances of God suggest that he has a body—rather, they demonstrate that, because he *doesn't* have a body, he can show himself in any way he chooses.

Christians everywhere believe that God is present with them. Some of us might have difficulty understanding how God can be in the United States at the same time he is in Korea or Nigeria. Although we can't offer a complete explanation of how this is possible, the realization that he doesn't have a body helps us understand that he can be present everywhere at once. He is not confined to any physical dimension, such as place.

Because this is so, God cannot be a local deity. Many ancient people thought that gods were regional, so each tribe or area had its own god. But this is a false teaching—God is a spirit, and therefore he is not restricted to any one geographical location.

Confusion About the Meaning of Spirit

It is not only people who embrace primitive pagan religions who are confused about God's spirituality. The fact that God is spirit also confuses many twentieth-century people. Modern man thinks that the idea of God's spirituality contradicts much of what he has learned about deciding if something is "for real." He would rather decide on the basis of its tangibility whether something exists. Can it be observed, touched, seen? It would seem that most people today are from Missouri, the "show me" state.

Many of us have adopted a similar mentality about God: "I'll believe he exists when you show him to me." And by that we mean that we will believe when we have some empirical evidence that he is real. Once a Soviet cosmonaut was asked if he had seen God. He replied that he hadn't seen God, and he concluded that God did not exist. This proved to be excellent propaganda for the atheist; but did it really say anything significant about whether God exists or not?

What is dangerous about such an outlook is that it reflects the way many people think. They are not at all interested in believing in God, simply because they cannot see him. What they are really doing is either to ignore, or to repudiate, the declaration in the Bible that God is a spirit.

But even when we are persuaded that God doesn't have a body, where do we go next? This is not an easy question to answer.

It should be clear by now that comparing God with people is of no help to us when we try to explain that God is spirit. Because he is a spirit, we can't say where he lives. Of course, when you talk with little children, they all know where God is—they will tell you that he lives in heaven. But that is just a linguistic shortcoming on our part; we know that God lives everywhere, heaven included.

Because God is a spirit, neither is he confined by time. He is not a God only of ancient or modern people; he is the God of people throughout history. God's spirituality helps us to explain how he could be present with Abraham in ancient Mesopotamia, with Paul in first-century Rome, or with us in the twentieth century, wherever we are. He is the God of people all over the world. Because God is spirit, he is able to transcend both time and space.

Even though we can't see God because he doesn't have a body, he does give us some evidence of his existence—we know that God acts. His actions leave obvious evidences of his existence. We've already reviewed some of those proofs in earlier chapters as we discussed such things as creation and salvation.

An Illustration of Spirit

If you had to explain to your children, or someone else's, what it means that God is a spirit, what would you say to them? Could you go beyond simply saying to them, "God does not have a body"?

The Bible does give us some help at this point. One biblical illustration that Jesus used is that of wind (John 3:8). We never see the wind; we only see evidences of it. We don't know where it begins, and we don't know where it ends. We do know when it comes by, because we feel it, or we see the leaves moving or the dust being blown. So it is with God. We don't see him, but we do see evidences of him.

Worshiping in Spirit

Many people from non-Christian religions are puzzled by our approach to worship, for they have no concept of God as spirit. They expect him always to be seen, to have a tangible existence. That is why they engage in the folly of using idols to worship.

For example, many of us worship in a building without any pictures. We claim to be worshiping God, and go there week after week and claim to be in the presence of God. But the amazing thing is that no one ever sees God. One's first impression might be that this doesn't make any sense. If we can't see him, how can he be there?

Actually, the fact that God is a spirit makes our claims about worship credible. If we used ordinary criteria for determining someone's presence or absence, it would seem obvious that God should always be visible to us; and if he is not visible, then we would assume he is not present. But we have learned not to compare God to people; and since he has plainly told us that he is a spirit, we are not to *expect* to see him. Thus the idea of God being spirit makes Christianity more sensible.

The Bible doesn't devote much time to describing what it means when it calls God *spirit*; it simply affirms—and assumes that we will understand—that he is a spirit. Part of that is due to the context into which the Bible was sent. People at that time in history had become accustomed to a God who was spirit.

In our modern setting, we like to think in terms of concrete, material things. We are uncomfortable thinking about non-material entities that we can neither control, nor hope to control, through technological means. The people of Jesus' day were not materialists in the same way many modern people are.

Perhaps one of the best ways to understand what the Bible means by saying God is spirit is to look at John 4, where his spirituality is clearly stated. In his conversation with the woman at the well, you'll remember, Jesus talked about her and about her sin. When he did so, she tried to change the subject and talk about religion. She wanted to know if the Jews or the Samaritans were correct in their teaching about the proper place for worship. In this context, Jesus told the woman that God is a spirit.

One of the questions Jesus answered is where people are to worship. Is it correct to worship only in Jerusalem, as the Jews say, or is it right to worship where the Samaritans do? Jesus made it very clear that the Jews were right. The Samaritans were wrong; they didn't know what they were doing.

God Is Not Confined to Space

But Jesus says that there is a time coming—and has now come—when true worshipers will worship in spirit and in truth. That is, they can worship God anyplace, *because* he is spirit. This is especially important to people in the Christian church who don't have Jewish antecedents, people who may not be comfortable talking about spirit. We can worship God anyplace because, as spirit, he is not confined to place.

John 4 makes it clear that, because God is spirit, he is to be worshiped in truth, which means that we can't use material objects such as idols in our worship. To do so would falsify our worship. God must be worshiped in a spiritual, noncorporeal way. We aren't to behave like the people who worship the Dalai Lama, or like the whirling dervishes. We don't have to engage in all sorts of ritual movement, as some feel constrained to do.

The Role of the Holy Spirit

We can go even further. To worship God in truth means that we must worship him in accordance with the Spirit. This is where the third person of the Trinity, the Holy Spirit of God, comes to bear on our worship. Our worship must be worship that is kindled in us—and drawn out of us—by the Holy Spirit. In his gospel, John was pointing out that the Holy Spirit ought to be functioning in our worship. God's Spirit, the Holy Spirit, works in us and leads us to worship.

Moreover, Paul tells how the Spirit works with us in prayer, helping us to pray, and in fact interceding for us (see Romans 8:26, 27).

Worshiping in truth means that we worship according to the truth God has given. The Holy Spirit is the giver of the Bible, and also the interpreter of it. If we worship in spirit, we worship in accordance with what the Spirit reveals to us.

This is one of the reasons why people in the Reformed tradition have been zealous to worship exclusively according to the Word of God. In Deuteronomy 12 we are forbidden either to add to, or to fall short of, worship as he has laid it out for us. This warning was necessary because of the character and nature of God.

We see the same theme repeated in the Old Testament antagonism toward idol worship. Because God is a spirit and is to be worshiped in a spiritual way, worshiping by means of an idol is untrue worship, false worship. The Old Testament anticipates the New Testament's teaching that God must be worshiped in spirit and in truth. Those who use idols in worship really denigrate God—they try to make him into something that he is not. To worship by using idols means changing the sovereign God of heaven and earth into an image made by man.

Spirit and Flesh

Some may think that they can explain the Bible's teaching that God is spirit by contrasting spirit with flesh. I'm not sure that I agree with the arguments they put forth. They emphasize the contrast between flesh and spirit found in many places in the New Testament. By this they mean that the flesh is corporeal—that is, having body or substance. This meaning *is* present in the Bible. For example, in both Testaments we can find flesh used to describe the corporeal (Genesis 40:19; Ephesians 2:15).

I believe that when the New Testament mentions *spirit*, it speaks primarily about the Holy Spirit. It strikes me that flesh is more of an ethical term, not having to do with metaphysics. That is, it is less of an explanation of what essentially constitutes something, and more of an assessment of whether it is good or bad. Therefore the contrast between spirit and flesh is basically a contrast between good and evil.

To summarize, we may say that God, as spirit, is one who does not have a body. When we speak thus about him, we must be careful that we don't think about him as some ghostly figure, someone who is not real, but rather imaginary. And he is not some sort of impersonal force; God, as spirit, has personality. One of the things we note about God is that he has feelings. The Bible talks about how we can grieve God and how God can be angry. When the Bible talks about God as spirit, we are compelled to see him as fully personal.

At the beginning of this chapter I referred to the Westminster Confession of Faith, which teaches that God does not have passions. This doesn't mean that God does not have feelings. Rather, it means that God is not governed by the things around him. (The word *passions* as it was used in that era had more to do with the description of how people reacted to their circumstances than it did with inner feelings.) What the framers of the

Confession were trying to say was, God is not a product of his circumstances; that is, his personality is not formed in reaction to anything around him. Indeed, the opposite is true: everything that exists comes as a result of God's action. This is significant as we think of God as spirit.

Consequences of God's Spirituality

There are some further consequences of God's being spirit that we ought to keep in mind. One is that we have to realize that, because God is spirit, he can dwell in our hearts. Another is that we can go into a room and worship him who is invisible. It is something that ought to remind us—and prompt us—to worship him. When we choose to forget that God is spirit, our worship is poverty-stricken.

Our daily lives are influenced by our belief in God as spirit. We can limit our fears, quell our passions, and remind ourselves of God's grace at any time of the day or night. We don't need to fear because, as spirit, he will never be far from us.

How does one go about serving the God who is spirit? Obviously we cannot do as some pagans do—provide him with food and drink, and thereby expect to win his favor. Such worship is sinful folly.

Spirit and Truth

Rather, we should prize worshiping God in spirit and truth. When we come before God in worship, we must remember that, since he is spirit, he can see into our hearts. He knows whether we are worshiping him with true love and zeal. He knows if our repentance is true, or just a show for our fellow worshipers. Most of us engage in sham worship at some time or another. Yet, because we recognize that God is spirit, we should realize that he will not accept such worship. Christians are obligated to offer true worship to God—worship that grows out of a pure and undefiled heart.

But how could we ever worship God in truth? We know we

are sinners, even when we are engaged in worship. Nevertheless, we *can* worship God. He is the one who makes our worship true, because he accepts those who acknowledge their sins. He sees them, not in their unrighteousness, but clothed in the righteousness of Jesus Christ.

Because God, as spirit, accepts our worship, we can love and worship him all the more. As he does so, our service of God helps us to recognize his love for us, which in turn encourages us to love him more—which will, in the end, lead us to more faithful service.

God is spirit. We cannot see him, but we know he exists. He constantly bears testimony to his existence by his work in our hearts. He has no physical hand to touch us; but we as Christians are sure that God the Spirit has touched our hearts. He has changed them from unresponsive to spiritually sensitive. And marvel of marvels, he even dwells in our hearts! Only the God who is spirit could do that.

Review Questions

1. What are some common confusions about what it means that God is spirit?
2. How does the illustration of the wind in John 3:8 explain *spirit?*
3. Why can God be worshiped in *any* geographical area?
4. How does God's being spirit explain some unique characteristics of Christian worship?
5. What makes idol worship so inconsistent with true worship?

Discussion Questions

1. How would you explain God's spirituality to a twentieth-century person who believes that anything that exists is tangible?
2. Review the order of worship from a local church, and show how God's spirituality helps to make sense of the different parts.

3. How would you answer someone who told you that, because God is spirit, he is less real?
4. How will the fact that God is not confined by time or place affect the way you carry on your life?

God Is Light

Light is something that is at once fascinating and common. We can go through weeks in our lives and never be conscious of the impact of light on us. We flick the switch, and the light goes on. We go to bed in the dark, and arise to the light of a new day. Nothing exciting or out of the ordinary.

Then one day we talk to a friend who has just had laser surgery. It's hard to believe that this powerful medical tool is just a concentrated beam of light. We can't imagine how it does the amazing things it does. Suddenly, light is no longer mundane and common; it is fascinating and mysterious.

Or perhaps you overhear a conversation about fascinating discoveries in physics. If you are like me, you probably don't understand much—if anything—of Einstein's theory of relativity, let alone some of these newer developments. Nevertheless, you realize that what light is, and the way it behaves, plays a significant role in the theory. Both the modern physicist and the ancient poet of the Old Testament are enamored with the idea of light. Both can sing the praises of light and recognize its unfathomable properties.

We know what light is: we see it all the time. When light eliminates darkness, it removes fear and offers comfort and hope. Without light, we are frightened. But when we have it, we take it for granted.

Because light affects our daily lives, the Bible's assertion that God is light can benefit our Christian life. Our ability to understand some of the parallels between the properties of light and the character of God are interesting and profitable.

When John the apostle asserted that God is light, he did so to remind his audience of two things that are extremely important to them: fellowship and joy. Not only were these matters important to the recipients of his letter, they are important also to twentieth-century Christians. Because God is light, it is possible for us to have fellowship with him—and hence with one another. And as a result of having fellowship, we can have complete joy (1 John 1:3–7).

We can experience the joy and fellowship of which John speaks only when we know who God is. For it is impossible to have fellowship with one about whom we know nothing. Because God is light, he makes himself known. And the illuminating character of light reminds us that God's self-revelation is clear to his people.

Note first of all that John compares the fact that God is light to other concepts. "This is the message we have heard from him and declare to you: God is light; in him there is no darkness at all" (1 John 1:5). When John describes God as light, he does so by contrasting him with darkness. In the Bible, darkness frequently symbolizes evil. Fundamentally, then, John's assertion that God is light communicates the idea that God is absolutely pure, righteous, holy and glorious. He is holy because there is no darkness—that is, no sin—in him.

God is light, and he is a pure light. God is truthful and pure; there is nothing about him that is untruthful or impure. There is nothing vicious, perverted or filthy about him. God is not only *not* any of these things, but his presence also exposes them. To be in the light is to live by the truth (1 John 1). If we claim that God is light, entailed also is a commitment to live according to his truth.

Light implies goodness, safety and life. Darkness, on the other hand, implies the opposite: falsehood, evil, sorrow, death. These things are perversions of God as light.

When we think of God as light in the physical realm, we

think of splendor and glory. In the intellectual realm, we think of truth. To be in the light—and to be warmed by it—means to have all of God's saving work bear fruit in our entire life.

The Function of Light

When we begin to understand the function of light, our understanding of who God is increases. One of the things that light brings is life—every gardener understands this. When there is more light during the summer, the plants grow fine; when there's less light, the plants don't grow as well. Every winter you are reminded of this when you look outside and see trees without leaves.

The Bible regularly relates light to life. For example, the phrase *light of life* appears in Job 33:30; Psalm 49:19; 56:13. When God created the world, he made the light; and from that flowed the rest of creation and all of life. John, in the first chapter of his gospel, reflects on the story of creation when he says of Jesus, "Through him all things were made; without him nothing was made that has been made. In him was life, and that life was the light of men" (John 1:3, 4).

Since God is light, he gives life. He did so when he created the world; but he also does so when he recreates us according to his grace. If we are to have fellowship with God, and complete joy, it is necessary for us to be alive. God, who is light, provides life for his people, and then allows them to have joyous fellowship with him and with each other.

God's saving, regenerating work among his people is a reminder that he is light. We have life—abundant life—because God, who is light, gives it. To be alive should be a reminder that we are able to enjoy fellowship with God. To avoid fellowship with God is to opt for death and darkness.

Light Illumines

Have you ever been in a completely dark place? Do you remember how difficult it was to recognize where you were?

You probably found it awkward, if not impossible, to find your way. Without light we are lost—in a sense, totally ignorant. But light illuminates and helps us to orient ourselves to our surroundings.

Without the illumining function of light, it would be impossible to have fellowship with God. As was mentioned above, God makes himself known because he is light; and knowing God is a prerequisite for fellowship and joy. But there is more to the truth that God is light than that he makes himself known. Because light illumines, it's possible to find our way.

I can recall a week at a summer Bible camp where I learned how important light was in directing me. My cabin was in the woods, and there were no lights at all nearby. One night I started out from my cabin to attend a meeting, and forgot to take my flashlight. I can remember stumbling and falling as I groped my way toward the main building. How grateful I was when Rick came up behind me with a flashlight! It was so easy to stay on the path then, without stumbling or falling. With a light on the path, I was able to get to my destination.

Because God is light, his word functions just as the flashlight did for me. As the psalmist says, his Word "is a lamp to my feet and a light for my path" (Psalm 119:105). Because God lights our path by his Word, it is possible for us to experience fellowship with him. He tells us how we are to do this, and makes clear to us the joy that results. As we read our Bibles and discover how to have a more intimate and joyous walk with God, we will discover what the apostle John means when he tells us that God is light.

One of the implications of the relationship between light and illumination pointed out above is that God wants us to know about him. Because God makes himself known, we should seek to receive that knowledge for ourselves. Furthermore, we should also learn what he requires of us, for God expects his people to obey him. That is why the Bible talks about walking in the light. We walk in obedience to God as he helps us to understand what he wants us to do for him. In so doing, we experience both joy and fellowship.

Light Overcomes Darkness

Not only does light illuminate, but it also drives out darkness. Where light shines, there cannot be darkness. Think of what it is like to be outside on a bright sunny day—the light of the sun eliminates darkness. On such days it is difficult to get out of the light of the sun. This is just a pale analogy of what the light of God is like.

Fellowship with God is a fellowship of light, not of darkness. "If we claim to have fellowship with him yet walk in the darkness, we lie and do not live by the truth" (1 John 1:6). God simply does not have fellowship with the darkness.

Light and Darkness

Therefore when John says that "God is light; in him there is no darkness at all" (1 John 1:5), he means that there is no evil in God. God is the opposite of evil; he is holy, pure and righteous. The notion that God is light indicates that God will not let evil continue; he overcomes it.

This is a significant part of what John was trying to communicate in his first letter. He showed that God overcame the evil of darkness by sending his Son, the Lord Jesus, to destroy sin *and* evil. This is one of the reasons why Jesus can be referred to as the light of the world.

In John's Gospel, light is frequently set over against the evil and corrupting influence of darkness. In Chapter 3 we are told that light came into the world and men hated the light and loved the darkness. The world's love of darkness is like being in a dark room, and someone turns on a very powerful light. What is your first reaction? You try to cling to the darkness. You close your eyes, or maybe you shield them from the light or cry out, "Turn off that light!" The reason the people of this world love the darkness is because their deeds are evil.

The same truth is found in 1 John 2:9. If we hate our brother, we are not in the light, but rather are still in the darkness. If we are in the darkness, then we will stumble. By contrast, the light keeps us from stumbling.

In John 3:19–21 we are told more about what light is and the way in which Jesus is that light. Light is not only connected with righteousness, it also has the quality of being able to expose darkness for what it is—namely, sin and evil. When Jesus came into the world, people disliked him because he witnessed to righteousness. They also despised him because he exposed them as unrighteous and evil. Since they loved darkness rather than light, they wanted to get away from the light. Eventually they tried to extinguish that light by destroying Jesus Christ.

Dealing with the Light

It is important for us to think about how we deal with God as light. There is something about light that has a separating character. Especially it can divide goodness from evil; when light exposes and illuminates things, people choose either to walk in the light or to cling to darkness and evil.

Because God is light, we not only see the true nature of things, but we also are forced to make choices between righteousness and unrighteousness. Because of our evil deeds, we often choose darkness. Tragically, not only do we hang on to our evil deeds, we shun the light of God, the light of Jesus.

The Light of the World

If we expect to have fellowship with God, we need to remember that we must walk in the light. God makes it possible to walk in the light through his Son, the Lord Jesus, the light of the world. The idea that Jesus is the light of the world is anticipated in the Old Testament:

> The people walking in darkness have seen a great light; on those living in the land of the shadow of death a light has dawned....For to us a child is born, to us a son is given, and the government will be on his shoulders. And he will be

called Wonderful Counselor, Mighty God, Everlasting Father, Prince of Peace....He will reign on David's throne and over his kingdom....The zeal of the LORD Almighty will accomplish this (Isaiah 9:2, 6, 7).

The above passage obviously refers to Jesus Christ, who came as the light of the world.

There came a man who was sent from God; his name was John. He came as a witness to testify concerning that light, so that through him all men might believe. He himself was not the light; he came only as a witness to the light. The true light that gives light to every man was coming into the world (John 1:6–9).

Here we have the witness of John the Baptist to the light who came into world. John came doing lots of things we associate with the light; but it is clear that he was not the light. He came calling people to righteousness and repentance. He proclaimed the coming of the light of the world, and bore witness to the fact that Jesus was that light. Finally—and in a climactic way—Jesus described himself: "I am the light of the world. Whoever follows me will never walk in darkness, but will have the light of life (John 8:12).

The joy and fellowship promised by John because God is light is ours because Jesus is the light of the world. He makes it possible for all his people to live in the light of God's presence, because he truly is the light who removes, conquers and absolutely destroys the darkness of sin and evil for us.

Light Is Inescapable

But what of those who choose darkness? They really seem to believe that they can escape the light, but they can't—ever! Calvin in his treatment of light points this out. He reminds us that, if people try to hide the light, it will reflect off something else. It has a quality that makes it impossible to eliminate or to extinguish. Christians themselves, as they are partakers of the light of God's countenance, reflect the light into the world. In so doing they expose the evil works of darkness and call attention to God as light.

> "You are the light of the world. A city on a hill cannot be hidden. Neither do people light a lamp and put it under a bowl. Instead they put it on its stand, and it gives light to everyone in the house. In the same way, let your light shine before men, that they may see your good deeds and praise your Father in heaven" (Matthew 5:14–16).

When we fellowship with the Father of lights and the Son who is the light of the world, then we become beacons ourselves. We are not the source of the light, but simply a reflection of the light. As such we expose evil deeds, lead others to recognize the true light, and encourage them to give glory to him. Only those who are experiencing fellowship with God can do this.

Light Is Good

When we as believers think of light, we seldom think of it negatively, but rather as something good. This is one of the characteristics of light portrayed in Scripture. So when the Bible says that God is light, it describes him as positive and benign. John makes this clear when he sets light over against darkness.

David wrote of his reliance on God as light in the first verse of Psalm 27: "The LORD is my light and my salvation—whom shall I fear?" Light drives away fear.

Isaiah 60 pictures the marvel of God's kingdom. In this chapter God is likened to light (verses 1, 19, 20). The coming of light will bring things such as gold, bronze, precious stones, etc. (verse 17). Where light is, sorrow will be driven away and righteousness will take its place (verses 20, 21). As we see something of the nature of light, we see something of the powerful and holy nature of God.

The prophet Micah tells us that Israel's enemies should not gloat over them anymore, because the Lord is light (Micah 7:8).

He who is light will expose Israel's sin; but will also plead the cause of his people, bringing to them the light of his justice. God's justice and light are tied together.

In Revelation 22:5, John tells us that God is the light who in heaven will make the sun and moon unnecessary. The servants of the Lord will be given light, and they will reign for ever and ever.

Paul explains to the church in 2 Corinthians 4:6 that the glory of God is seen in the face of Jesus. Paul is alluding to what happened at creation, where God said, "Let there be light," and there was light. Just as God made the light at creation, he makes known his glory through his Son, the Lord Jesus. Paul says that the light shines in our hearts to give us this knowledge.

Acknowledging the Light

When we turn on the light in a dark room, we are able to avoid things that could harm us. Likewise, when we acknowledge that God is light, the sin that is all around us is exposed. We benefit from the fact that God is light by avoiding that which is contrary to light, such as sin and evil.

Light also shows us what our sins have been in the past. It doesn't undo those sins; but when we acknowledge and confess them before God, he forgives us. He also cleanses us— that's another benefit of the fact that God is light. We should be moved to gratitude as we understand that God has removed our sins from us.

In James 1:17 we are told that God is dependable, a quality having to do with his covenant faithfulness. As the Father of heavenly lights, he doesn't change like a shifting shadow.

Walking in the Light

How can we love and serve God, who is light? The first thing we can do is to walk in the light. This means we have to walk in fellowship with God. Many of us think we are too busy to walk with God; it has a fairly low priority. That's almost like trying to switch off the benefits of light! Instead, we should take advantage of the opportunities to fellowship with God and to bask in his light.

Something else is necessary if we are to walk in the light: we must follow the path that God has set before us. Remember my story about trying to walk through the woods without a light? Stumbling was easy—I needed a light on the path; and when it was there, I had to follow it. The same thing happens to us if we don't walk in the light: we trip and stumble. Then we end up injured by sin and evil.

John 2:9 shows us some concrete ways to walk in the light. The apostle tells us that we can know whether we're walking in the light by the way we treat other people. This is particularly true as we relate to other Christians. John says that if we see that our brother needs something that we have and don't give it to him, we aren't loving our brother—we're not walking in the light.

Light and Love

Because God is light, we ought to love the light. We ought to enjoy the way in which we are enlightened by God. We ought to love the word he gives us, and the work of his Spirit in our hearts. There ought to be a real joy from studying the Word of God. We ought to rejoice in being the recipients of the Word; it ought to count in our lives.

We also need to love the holiness and righteousness of God. That's not easy: most of us have a natural tendency *not* to want to get too close to holiness and righteousness. A little is alright, but too much goes too far. Sometimes we shy away from people who are righteous. But we must learn to really love these characteristics of God portrayed in his people.

In our society, it is easy to become inoculated against evil to the point where it doesn't bother us at all. We can take large doses of it without being upset. But God, who is light, exposes such folly. He shows us the way back to him. He reminds us to love him who is light. In so doing, he leads us to serve him according to his light in his Word.

Review Questions

1. What does the apostle John mean when he says there is no darkness in God?
2. What does the truth that light brings life indicate about the character of God?
3. How does God, as light, carry out his illuminating functions?
4. What is Jesus' role as the light of the world?
5. Why can the light of God be described as inescapable?

Discussion Questions

1. What characterizes a person who walks in the light? Do *you* have these characteristics? If not, what must you do to acquire them?
2. What does the inescapable character of light mean for Christian witness?
3. How does the fact that God is light encourage the Christian to be holy?
4. How does the Word of God help you to walk in the light? Are you satisfied with your walk? How should you change?
5. Which of the analogies of light is most helpful to you in your Christian walk? Explain.

God Is Love

JENNIE LOVES BILL. She wants to spend time with him, talk with him, watch him while he practices. Even though she is only a high school senior, she knows this is the real thing. Her parents aren't quite so sure. They caution her that true love could easily be confused with many other emotions.

Nevertheless, Jennie persists in her protestation that she is in love with Bill. After all, she reasons, he makes me feel so good, and he's so *popular*. Why wouldn't she love the captain of the football team? When she had started to date Bill, her entire life changed. Bill had made it all happen for her.

Bill claims to love Jennie just as much as she loves him. Bill has trouble talking to people, but around Jennie he never experiences any such difficulty. Bill is purposeful: he seldom, if ever, relaxes. But Jennie has a soothing effect on him. Sure, Bill loves Jennie—what else could make him feel so good when he is with her?

You may be thinking "adolescent infatuation"—that's all there is to it. But can you be *sure?* Why would you say that they're not really in love—is it their *age?* Is it the way they *describe* their love?

The story could be changed to fit an older couple; but would that make it easier to tell if they were really in love? Twentieth-century people find it difficult to talk about love, because they don't have a good idea what it really is.

Our ignorance not only clouds our judgments about personal relationships, it also weakens our understanding of the character and nature of God.

Contemporary Views of Love

Is love self-giving, or self-satisfaction? Is it a feeling, or a rational passion? Is love something that makes *me* feel good, or is it making *someone else* feel good?

Arriving at a clear definition of love in our contemporary cultural context is difficult, because of all such competing definitions around us. For many of us, love is a feeling. We also confuse love and lust in our society. And romance and infatuation can be mistaken for love.

But when we look at love in the Bible, it is much more. When the Bible defines love, it concentrates on the needs of others rather than on ourselves. By contemporary definitions of love, concern for others is frequently lacking. Note, in the story of Bill and Jennie, how each knew they were in love because of what they received in the relationship.

John's Description of God's Love

God is concerned that his people understand what love is, because he is love. In order to understand what love is and something of the nature and character of God, it is helpful to focus on 1 John 4. John tells us in this chapter that God is love (verses 8, 16).

If there is one characteristic of God that most people today agree on, it is that he is love. This contention will not generate a lot of controversy. Nevertheless, we must not allow the noncontroversial nature of the statement that God is love to lull us into believing that all people mean the same thing by it. Christians must be careful to derive their understanding of "God is love" from the Bible, not from the confused and erroneous ideas about love that surround them today.

We must pay attention to the things that are fairly obvious

from John's letter. God's love is defined primarily in terms of what he does. He exercised his love when he sent his Son to die in the place of his people. This is the focal point of John's explanation of the fact that God is love.

John argues that, in order for us to know God, we must love God—and vice versa. "Everyone who loves has been born of God and knows God. Whoever does not love does not know God, because God is love" (verses 7, 8).

Love and Knowledge

John relates love to knowledge because the character of our understanding of God is experiential. This does not mean that experiential knowledge has no factual or cognitive elements. We must not assume that our information about God comes to us apart from the facts about his existence and personality, as revealed to us in the Bible. Rather, he has made sure that the record of his dealings with men has been preserved down through the ages.

We must recognize that God's revelation of himself is addressed to our minds and understanding. It does not require us to stop thinking, and simply feel. This is especially true if we want to understand his love.

But the knowledge of God that John talks about goes beyond mere cognition: it has another distinctive component. This experiential nature of knowing God can be understood by looking at some analogies.

Try to imagine how you could come to understand or explain the color yellow without experiencing it. You may be able to give a scientific explanation about the color of light on the spectrum as seen through a prism; but would you really know what yellow was? Or you could give a more poetic definition of yellow as a mild or pleasing color. But again, would you understand what it meant that something was yellow? Of course not. In order to understand what yellow is, you must experience it. You must see something that is that color, and contrast it with things that are not yellow. Then you could understand what it meant to call something yellow.

Knowing God and loving God are similar. If you don't know him, you can't comprehend what is meant when it is said that God is love. You need to experience God's love in order to know what it is.

Trying to understand God's love would be like trying to describe vanilla ice cream without ever tasting it. You might tell someone that vanilla doesn't taste like chocolate, but that would not satisfy. Or you could say that it is delicious and pure. You could describe it as an exciting and refreshing taste. You may even go so far as to say that it is one of the most pleasing sensations ever experienced by man. But would anyone really know what vanilla ice cream was, after these descriptions? Vanilla ice cream must be experienced to know what it is. You need to slide it into your mouth and savor it on your tongue if you are going to know what vanilla ice cream truly is.

John is saying something similar. In order to know God, we must experience him. The way we experience him is to love. We must both give and receive love in order to know God.

But you ask, Why must I love in order to know God? Because the Bible answers—God is love.

Love Belongs to the Essence of God

We can know God by loving because love belongs to the essence of God. It is an aspect of God that, once acquired, enables us to know something of God. For example: We could liken the way in which God's love belongs to his essence in the same way that certain distinctive odors belong to foods. Think of an onion and you think of its distinctive aroma. Or you are aware that you don't need to see cabbage to know that it is cooking on the stove—you can smell it. These aromas belong to the essence of onions and cabbage, and when we smell them we know what they are.

We know something of God when we experience love,

because God is love. It can be no other way. When we receive love, or when we love others, we are able to recognize something that belongs to the essence of God—his love.

Love is Impossible Apart from God

We must acknowledge that love cannot be acquired apart from God, for we cannot love or know him without his gracious activity. Don't be deceived into thinking that anyone who shows love is somehow able to know God. This is not the case, as many examples from the Bible testify.

If someone shows what we think is love, and we discover that he doesn't love God, then we have a counterfeit. In fact, there are many cases of false love around. Some people think that lust is love; others believe that doing nice things for someone else is love. They perform their acts of kindness totally devoid of any sense of who God is. We must not be tricked— God is the source of love. We can truly love only as we love him, because he is love.

John proceeds to show us that if we don't love, then we don't know God. "Whoever does not love does not know God, because God is love" (1 John 4:8). Without love we remain ignorant of God. Because he is love, and allows us to experience that love, we will find it impossible to know God if we fail to love. This can help us today, just as it helped people in John's day. If someone does not love his neighbor, then it must be that he is ignorant of God.

John also supports the contrary idea: that if we love, then we can know God. Therefore, we should be *sure* that we love one another. If we do, this should be a tremendous encouragement to us; for if we do good to our brothers and sisters for the right reasons, then we know God.

God's Great Act of Love

John further defines what it means that God is love by explaining God's greatest act of love. "This is how God showed

81

his love among us; He sent his one and only Son into the world that we might live through him" (1 John 4:9). We should first note that God did not send his Son because of our love. This is not a quid pro quo situation, where God does something because he feels obligated. The Bible is clear that God did not love because we first loved him—he is not obligated to return a favor, so to speak. We do not even *incline* God to show his favor to us because we love him or our brothers or sisters. The sole and simple reason why God has shown his love to us is because God is love.

God sent his Son into the world so that we could live in him. Because God so loved us, says John in his Gospel (3:16), he sent his Son. The sending of his Son into the world is a demonstration of God's love.

Many fail to recognize that the sending of Jesus into the world was a loving act. If we forget the character of this world into which Jesus came, or the place from which he came, we will not see the incarnation as an act of love. Jesus had experienced the glories of heaven, with all the pleasures that legitimately belong to the second person of the Godhead. And the most important of these had been fellowship with his righteous and holy Father.

But God sent his Son to live on the earth. He sent the Son, who was active in creation, to dwell with *creatures*. Even more humiliating was the fact that God sent his Son into a *sinful* world. The holy one of God came to dwell in the midst of sinful, unholy people! He who gave the law sent his Son to reside with lawbreakers. Jesus, the only true fount of good, came to live with men and women who are evil and vile.

Furthermore, Jesus came to earth and lived a life of perfect obedience to the law of God. He fulfilled the law in order that we might be made righteous in him.

Atoning Love

"This is love: not that we loved God, but that he loved us and sent his Son as an atoning sacrifice for our sins" (1 John

4:10). Jesus came to earth, and lived a completely holy and righteous life. For that demonstration of holiness his fellow countrymen crucified him. They put him to death for the honest claims he made. They put him to death for his righteousness.

But not only under the hand of cruel men did Jesus suffer: he suffered also at the hands of the perfect Judge. He experienced the wrath of God against sinners. He felt total alienation from his Father when he experienced the ignominy of the crucifixion.

At this you might break out in a chant—Why, why, why? The answer is in the three little words of 1 John 4: *God is love.*

John tells us that God is love, and then shows us how God exercised that love. He gave his most precious possession, his only Son, because he is love. The loving God is the one who gives of himself for the benefit of others. When we try to imagine what the Bible means when it says that God is love, we need only think about what he did when he sent his only begotten Son into the world.

God's Love is Compatible with His Justice

Because God is love does not mean that he is not also many other things. A lot of people in our society think that because God is love he can't be anything else. Some, for example, think that if God is love, then he cannot be just. Many people say that he will never send anyone to hell, because he is love. The Bible takes the contrary point of view: God is just, and *must* send sinners to hell. But because he loves his people, he punished his Son, the Lord Jesus, in their place so that they will not go to hell.

Anyone who has ever dealt with young children can see the way in which love and justice must mesh. If a child does something wrong, the most loving thing a parent can do is to allow him to suffer the just consequences of his act. I can remember taking something from a friend's home one time, and my parents found out what I had done. Because they loved me, they made me return the item and suffer the humiliation that accompanied my sin. They loved me and made sure that justice prevailed. It would have been much easier for them, and certainly for me, if we had forgotten about the insignificant item. But because of their love, they made me learn an important lesson—the lesson of justice. These two characteristics are not incompatible; they are necessarily related to each other.

One problem we have to confront in defining love is to decide whether we can say that love is always other-directed. If we define love in that way, can we include God in the definition? Is it not the case that God does things for his own glory? Didn't God make everyone for his own good pleasure? If we define love exclusively as directed toward others, can we include in our definition what God does? These are the hard problems that need to be dealt with in dealing with the realization that God is love. He demonstrated his love in sending Jesus to die for his people; and so, on the basis of what John tells us, we can and must include what God does in our definition of love. God is love!

Some people claim that because God is love, he couldn't stoop to administer punishment. They want to call God *Love*, and nothing else. This is not what John is saying here. There are other things that characterize the nature of God besides love. God doesn't stop being love only because he is just and eventually punishes people. We don't have to say that since God is one he cannot be the other.

One aspect of God's love is that he is merciful. In order for us to understand mercy, we have to set it over against judgment. How can he be merciful if there is no possibility of judgment?

When we talk about love, we have to see that somehow love and punishment go together. Because you engage in punishment doesn't mean that love stops. Sometimes, as a matter of fact, punishment *results* from God's love. We see this in Proverbs 12, where we learn that God chastens the ones he loves. Thus punishment is an evidence of God's love.

Relationship between the Father, Son and Holy Spirit

God demonstrates that he is love in yet another way: in the intertrinitarian relationships. At the time of his baptism and on the Mount of Transfiguration, Jesus is described as the one whom God loves. This is a part of the relationship between the Father and the Son. Jesus also tells us that he loves the Father. In these relationships, we see something of the character and nature of God: he is love. The Father loves the Son and the Holy Spirit, and each of them loves the Father and one another. God's love touches all of his relationships—it's not confined simply to his creatures.

In 1 John 4, the apostle is trying to convince people to love one another. In verse 7 he pleads, "Dear friends, let us love one another." The source of that love is God's love. John makes it clear that the way in which we come to have love is to acquire it from God. In fact, our love for one another is to mirror the loving relationship among the members of the Trinity.

Loving God and Loving Others

God has demonstrated his love by loving us before we loved him—in fact, he loved us when we were unlovely. He didn't wait for us to reciprocate. This should help us to understand something about the character of God's love. It is in clear contrast to the love that we find in the world. God's love does not depend on our responding to him. God's love is unconditional—it is not based on anything we do.

Even though God's love doesn't depend on reciprocal arrangements, once it is in gear it has to have an effect upon us. It enables and requires us, on our part, to love. This love is to be exercised toward God and also toward others. What John is trying to show us is that, if love toward God is absent, we really don't understand what God's love is, and really don't know God. It would also mean that God had never set his love upon us, that we have never been the recipients of his love. This is one of the characteristics of God's love, and John is zealous that we be clear about it.

John also tells us that love drives away fear (1 John 4:18). The reason we no longer have to fear is that we are delivered from the judgment, the final condemnation that comes upon all mankind. Perfect love therefore drives out all fear.

After John has given his arguments for God as love, he returns to the main issue: If we don't have the right relationship of love with our brother, then we've missed the whole point. We don't understand what it really means that God is love. For God is loved and served as we help those in need.

Review Questions

1. What are some common ways that people define love?
2. What does it mean to say that love belongs to God's essence?
3. What is the relationship between loving God and knowing God?
4. What makes Christ's incarnation such a great act of love?
5. What are some evidences that you truly know and love God?

Discussion Questions

1. Is love, for you, self-*giving* or self-*satisfying*? Explain.
2. Do you see any incompatibility between God's love and God's justice? Explain. Discuss examples of punishment as a demonstration of love.
3. How can you tell if you have experienced God's love?
4. What are ways that you, as an individual or as a member of Christ's church, can love your brothers and sisters?
5. When you meditate on God's love, does it move you to do anything? If so, what?

God Is Triune

WHEN CHRISTIANS TALK ABOUT THE TRINITY, they are talking about God as three-in-one, or one-in-three. Longtime members of the church talk about God as triune with a fair degree of frequency and ease. Some of us sing from *Trinity Hymnal* and attend Trinity Church. Although Christians are comfortable with the word *Trinity*, when it comes to explaining the fine details of what it means—that God is triune—many find it a bit more difficult. The clear distinctions and definitions we are required to make are not easy.

Any discussion of the Trinity uses theological language that helps us make sense out of biblical teaching. For you see, the Bible never uses the word *Trinity*. There is no one proof text that tells us that God is One and God is Three, or that explains the details of the Trinity. In order to make sense of the theological concept of the Trinity, we need to pull together a lot of biblical evidence. Only then can we develop a clear understanding of this teaching.

A Historical Perspective

Through the years, the church has sought to make sense out of the biblical evidence about the nature of God. It took the church quite a while in its early history to formulate the doctrine of the Trinity. Church historians argue that the trinitarian controversies characterized the early church more strongly than any other issue did.

Once the church accepted the doctrine of the Trinity, they maintained it. Throughout the history of the church, some have denied this biblical doctrine, but clearly they are a minority. No segment of the Christian church has persistently denied the Trinity. There have been many aberrations, but those who deny the Trinity have eliminated themselves from any connection with what has historically been called Christianity.

The Trinity in the Old Testament

The doctrine of the Trinity is a New Testament doctrine. This doesn't mean that it is taught only in the New Testament, but it is primarily there.

Of course, there are intimations about the Trinity in the Old Testament. But it is the full revelation of God in the New Testament that helps us to understand the doctrine.

Monotheism characterized the worship of Old Testament Israel. The belief in one God set the Jews off from all the nations around them. For example, it distinguished them from the Egyptians, who worshiped not only cows but other things. The Israelites' Canaanitish neighbors also worshiped false gods, each of which did special things. And so, more than any other aspect of their national existence, the worship of the one true God set Israel apart from her neighbors.

Because faith in one God was so important in the Old Testament, we must be careful that we don't develop an understanding of the Trinity that is incompatible with that belief. Indeed, no New Testament teaching about God may be seen as contradictory to the Old Testament. Some non-Christians accuse believers of denying the unity of God that the Old Testament teaches. Clearly this is a false accusation. Nevertheless, we must make sure that our understanding of the Trinity complements all that the Old Testament teaches about God.

In the first chapter of the Bible, for example, God says, "Let us make man in our image, in our likeness" (Genesis 1:26). Why are the words *us* and *our* used here? Does the fact that God refers to himself in the plural contradict all of the rest of the Old Testament?

Similar language is found in other sections of the Old Testament; for example, in the incident at the tower of Babel: "Come, let us go down and confuse their language so they will not understand each other" (Genesis 11:7). God's reference to himself in the plural doesn't *prove* the Trinity, but it does tell us there is something special about the unity and plurality of God.

Genesis 18 records the incident of the Lord's visit to Abraham. The angel of the Lord appeared as three visitors, and the text refers to them as LORD (Genesis 18:13, 14). Here again, the language reflects something of the unity and plurality of the Godhead.

Some Old Testament discussions of the coming of the Messiah use language that reflects the diversity of God. In Isaiah 61:1f., similar language conveys something of the unity, diversity and plurality in the Godhead. Here Isaiah describes the work of the Messiah, the Promised One and the Prophet, and attributes to him all the characteristics of God. A number of other references in Isaiah show us the same thing. So, even though the Old Testament concentrates on the unity of the Godhead, it also presents the diversity of God as well (cf. Isaiah 48:16).

The Trinity Revealed in the New Testament

The New Testament expands on the Old. It maintains the doctrine of oneness and diversity, but elaborates on diversity to a much greater degree. One of the most obvious things that the New Testament teaches is that the Father has sent the Son into the world. In this connection, we see clearly the active engagement of the first two persons of the Trinity.

John's Gospel describes not only the work of the Father and the Son, but also the sending of the Holy Spirit. In John 14, Jesus tells his disciples that he is going to leave them, but they are not to fear, because he will send another Counselor—namely, the Holy Spirit. Thus John, in speaking of all three persons of the

Trinity, builds further upon the Old Testament foundation of God as pluralistic.

Other parts of the New Testament demonstrate the same point, as in Luke 3:22, where the Father addresses the Son at Jesus' baptism, and Luke 9:35, where his voice is again heard by those who witnessed the transfiguration. Here the diverse multi-person character of the Godhead comes out clearly. Obviously there were at least two persons of the Trinity present at both of these incidents. And in Romans 8:26 and 27 we are told that the Holy Spirit is the one who intercedes for us. The Holy Spirit, the third person of the Trinity, is able to speak to the Father, the first person of the Trinity.

There are also places in the New Testament where the Father, Son and Holy Spirit are spoken of in the same passage. For example, Paul does this in his benediction (2 Corinthians 13:14) and Jesus himself uses the same language in the baptismal formula in the Great Commission (Matthew 28:19).

The Old Testament emphasizes the oneness of God. Yet this oneness hints at the plurality of the Godhead. In the New Testament, God is referred to as God the Father, God the Son and God the Holy Spirit. To each member of the Trinity belong certain distinctives and roles. Each of the three persons has a unique relationship with the other two, and each has his particular tasks to carry out.

The Unity of the Godhead

We should note that the Father has all the characteristics of God. This is something that is never questioned—he is always called *God*.

So too is Jesus the Son, whom the New Testament portrays as having all the characteristics of God. The Scriptures are filled with evidence that show the divinity of Jesus Christ. He thinks of himself as divine, his actions demonstrate his divinity, and the teachings of the New Testament repeatedly show him to possess the attributes of God.

The New Testament makes it clear that the Holy Spirit is

also God. He has godly attributes, carries out godly actions, and is called *God* (Acts 5:3, 4).

The Diversity of the Godhead

Sometimes in the Bible we see God as Father, sometimes we see God as the Son, and sometimes we see God as the Holy Spirit. They are all one God, and yet they are each individually God.

It was left to the early church to try to bring all of these things together into some clear and positive formulation. Christians in those early years set forth clearly that God was one. We, like them, have to maintain the doctrine that God is the one true God.

We must also remember that the oneness of God is different from any other kind of oneness. This one God is three distinct persons, namely: the Father, the Son and the Holy Spirit.

When we use the word *persons*, we have to be very careful that we don't misconstrue it. We must make sure that we don't use the idea of *person*s to think of spatial differences. If I'm a person and you're a person, and there is space or time between us, we can't be one. Neither the New Testament nor the early church used the word *person* in such a way. Each person in the Trinity has his own characteristics, yet together they continue to be one God.

The Equality of the Godhead

It is impossible to explain exactly how this unity and diversity came about. All that we can say is that the Bible teaches us that there is one God, and that there are three persons in the Godhead. They aren't separated, they are a unity. We can't comprehend or explain it fully, but we accept it as what the Bible teaches.

We must remember that the attributes that belong to the oneness of God also belong to each of the persons of the Godhead. We cannot say that God the Father has something that is lacking in the Son or the Holy Spirit. That would not be true at all: the essence of God is found in each of the three persons of the Trinity. Each of them is completely and fully God. Each has the same divine characteristics.

We have to be careful also that we don't subordinate any one person of the Trinity to another. It would be improper to think of God the Father as the leader or captain, God the Son as a sort of lieutenant and the Holy Spirit as the private. The three persons of the Godhead are not to be distinguished by rank. If God the Father is a captain, so also is God the Son and God the Holy Spirit.

There are, however, some relationships between the three that we can't forget. They have mostly to do with the way in which the three persons in the Trinity work together. God the Father exercises fatherly functions and, as the Father, doesn't proceed from any of the others. The Son, because he is a son, proceeds from the Father. Theologians have talked about the Father as one who is neither begotten by, nor does he proceed from, another. The Son is begotten eternally. There was not a time when he started—he always *was*. It's not something that has to do with time, but with relationships.

Both the Father and the Son send the Holy Spirit. Theologians talk about the Holy Spirit as eternally proceeding from the Father and the Son. This has to do only with relationships between the members of the Trinity—it has nothing to do with time. Because this is an eternal relationship, the Holy Spirit has always proceeded from the Father and the Son—there was never a time when this relationship did not prevail. This eternal relationship does not mean that Jesus could not send a Counselor, the Holy Spirit (see John 16:5–15), for God's people experienced such a sending at Pentecost. But the proceeding of the Holy Spirit from the Father and the Son sets forth their relationship to one another for all eternity.

In the Old Testament, the primary focus was to help people understand who God the Father was. That doesn't mean that there was no Son or Holy Spirit at that time: it just wasn't the purpose of the Old Testament to emphasize the work of the second and third persons of the Trinity. It emphasized who God the Father was. In the Gospels the emphasis is upon God the Son. He takes center stage, and the revelation concentrates on who he is. The Gospels help us in a particular way to understand the nature and character of the second person in the Trinity.

At Pentecost, God ushered in the final part of his written revelation, which highlights the person and work of God the Holy Spirit. The book of Acts, as well as the Epistles, center on his particular work. It is not that God the Holy Spirit hadn't been functioning and acting before this period: it's just that, at this point in history, God decided to open this part of his revelation to us.

It is easy to confuse the various strains of biblical teaching on the Trinity. But we should try to understand, not only the relationships within the Trinity, but also the attributes that characterize each of the three persons of the Godhead.

The Mystery of the Trinity

Throughout the ages, the church has confessed that the doctrine of the Trinity is a mystery. Try as we might, we're not going to be able to tie up every loose end. (Nor are we going to be able to master completely everything else there is to know about the Triune God.) But we must constantly strive to bring together all the different aspects of the biblical revelation about the Trinity. As we struggle to understand what the Bible teaches, we acknowledge that our intellects are incapable of mastering all the aspects of our great God's being.

Even though the doctrine of the Trinity is complex and difficult to understand, there are a number of analogies that various teachers have used to help to explain the Trinity. Like all analogies, they have their weaknesses, yet they are useful in helping Christians better to understand what the historic doctrine of the Trinity means.

One of the simplest is the analogy of water. Water is always H_2O. But sometimes it is in the form of ice, sometimes it has a liquid form, and at other times it is steam. H_2O in all these various forms remains water. The different manifestations never change its basic character. We recognize and acknowledge that water is water in any of its forms—frozen, liquid, or vapor. While this analogy falls far short of fully explaining the Godhead, it may be helpful as to one characteristic of the Trinity: God continues to be God, just as water continues to be H_2O in each of its forms.

Responding to God's Character

Christians shouldn't be satisfied simply to study the doctrine of the Trinity just to get a better intellectual grasp of the biblical evidence. Of course, that's an important goal, but we should be able to go beyond intellectual cognition. In distinctively Christian ways, we ought to react to what the Bible teaches about the Triune God. One of our immediate reactions to the fact that God is triune should be awe. A God who has this kind of character—one whose person it is so intellectually demanding to understand—could well push our minds to the breaking point. We can't comprehend everything about the Trinity, nor can we control anything that the triune God does. Therefore we ought to rejoice in his greatness and marvel at his character.

We would do well to remember also that, in the Old Testament, people had such a small part of what we have—they didn't have anything like the fullness of revelation that we enjoy. Yet they were servants of the living God, and the quality of their service was astonishing. Look how Moses, Elijah and Elisha worshiped and served God. It's amazing how they were able—without seeing all the things that we see—to love and serve God so fully.

The same thing was true of those who followed Jesus during the early years of the Christian church. They were ignorant of many of the truths we now possess, but they willingly followed and served the Lord Jesus in ways that shame contemporary Christians. Since we live in a period when God's revelation is complete, isn't it to be expected that we would worship and serve him more fully than they? Without the fullness of revelation that we enjoy, they faithfully served and worshiped God.

Yet it seems that Christians in our day and age appear to be serving him less zealously than those in less privileged eras.

The doctrine of the Trinity is not some theological abstraction designed only for scholars and academics. Every believer should recognize the effect and impact of God's character on our daily lives.

Remember, each person of the Trinity is active in bringing about our salvation. Each plays an active and necessary role in saving us. Without all three, we would not be the people of God.

The Role of the Father

There are specific tasks that each of the three persons of the Trinity carries out in the accomplishment of salvation. Sometimes Scripture refers to God the Father as the creator of the whole earth (1 Corinthians 8:6 and Ephesians 3:14, 15). The name *Father* can also refer to God's special relationship to the children of Israel (Deuteronomy 32 and Isaiah 63 and 64). The Bible describes God's relationship to his people Israel as that of children to father.

The New Testament applies the term *father* to the relationship that God has to his people. Conversely, Christians are declared to be children of God or children of the Father. We recognize this in the Lord's Prayer.

God's special relationship to his people is more fully defined than just Creator. God the Father's particular work in redemption is that of election in the Son.

The Role of the Son

Sometimes *Son* is used in a metaphysical sense in terms of Jesus' relationship to the Father in the divine Trinity. The way in which he is the Son of God is not exactly the same as the way we are the sons of God. His relationship to the Father has different characteristics from our relationship to the Father.

Specifically, in the work of redemption the second person of the Trinity made atonement—that is, made us right with God.

He bore in his own body the just punishment for our sins. Because he had identified with his people, he bore the punishment their sin deserved.

The Role of the Holy Spirit

Like the Father and the Son (although not designated by familiar family terms, as are they), the Holy Spirit is deeply involved both in revelation and redemption. As the third person of the Trinity, he is not to be thought of as just some unidentifiable, mystical power—he is a *person*. We err seriously when we refer to the Holy Spirit as *it*. We would not refer to the Father or Jesus in that manner, and neither should we speak so of the Holy Spirit.

The Holy Spirit oversaw and preserved the writing of the Scriptures. Today he applies the teaching of that same Word to our lives. He knows whereof he speaks.

In the work of redemption, he actively related the work of the Father and of the Son to individual believers. We who are in the New Testament church ought to be especially aware of the leading and guiding functions of the Holy Spirit in our lives. He works and lives in our hearts by bringing to bear on all of us what the Scriptures teach. And he is the down payment (the guarantee) that God has given us that he will bring to completion all of his work.

Evaluating Our Response

Again, the doctrine of the Trinity is not easy to understand. Nevertheless, the difficulty we have in comprehending a small portion of what it means that God is three-in-one should remind us how great our God is. As you wrestle with the intellectually demanding work of trying to understand something of God's unity and diversity, remember that this great God—Father, Son and Holy Spirit—has bound himself to his people. His greatness should be apparent as you think of the complexity of the Godhead.

Therefore, we should honor him with our worship and service. But at the same time, we should remember that this great God has chosen to make himself known, not only to the brilliant and learned, but also to the faithful and trusting. Yes, God is complex and beyond our comprehension. Nevertheless, he receives worship from the simplest believers and rejoices in their service. We make sure that we render our praise and adoration, our work and service, our love and affection, to him and to him alone.

Review Questions

1. Define concisely the meaning of the term *Trinity*.
2. Cite Old Testament references to the Trinity.
3. Cite New Testament references to the Trinity.
4. Explain the meaning of unity and diversity.
5. Explain concisely how each member of the Trinity is involved in bringing about our salvation.

Discussion Questions

1. Discuss the importance of correctly understanding the Trinity. (You may focus on a particular person of the Trinity, such as the Son. Why is it crucial to understand that he is God?)
2. Why is it not possible, or necessary, for us to comprehend completely the Triune Godhead?
3. Discuss what it means for one member of the Trinity to proceed from another. Why is this important?
4. Discuss common misconceptions that lead to a depersonalization of the Holy Spirit.
5. Evaluate your response to the awesome wonders of our great God, who is mindful of each one who loves him. Are you truly worshiping him? How could you worship him better?

God Is Holy

WE LIVE IN A PROFANE ERA. You see it in the way we use language. Many of us are embarrassed because of the type of words that have become commonplace among Americans. The media no longer hesitate to take the name of the Lord in vain, or to engage in the use of the grossest vulgarities.

Not only do we hear this in the media, we also find it in common discourse. Those of you who work in offices and other places are probably horrified to hear locker-room language on the lips of well-educated men and women. Our schools have not escaped: since the 1960s there has been an increasing use of profane language, not just among students but also from teachers. I was shocked, when I went back for graduate study after a number of years out of college, to hear that kind of language in use by both students and professors.

The profane character of the present era is clearly evident in our literature. Today's popular authors not only use language that shocks, they also deal with topics in a profane and obscene way. Many contemporary novels and stories seem to need at least a minimum amount of indecency, in order to be considered salable items.

Profanity has also triumphed in the arts. There are many painters, sculptors and others who view their art as a means of liberating us from the constraints of a Christian worldview. The sacred, the holy—even the good—are parodied in movies and paintings. And often the music of our age does not reflect the nobility of man, but his depravity.

The Fear of Holiness

We Christians, living in such an age, frequently find holiness to be an unpleasant topic of conversation. We are uncomfortable when we are around people and things that convey holiness. Just as we are sometimes embarrassed by sleaze, we are uncomfortable with holiness. Think about how you feel right now. It was all right to condemn profanity, but to talk about holiness is probably not the antidote you have in mind. Some of you may even begin to squirm.

You teens—and those of you who can remember your teens—know the feeling. There is a similarity to the times when you had to be in the presence of your family and your friends at the same time. You weren't exactly ashamed of your parents, but you felt that you would like to distance yourself from them and get closer to your peers. Some of you may feel the same way about holiness.

Holiness is also a frightening topic: it conjures up in our minds visions of fire and destruction. We think about the profanity of our age and the impurity of our thoughts, and we are scared. The holiness of God is frightening to sinful people— and well it ought to be.

Nevertheless, we need to deal with the topic of holiness. The Bible emphasizes it, so we shouldn't try to avoid it. In fact, in order truly to know who God is, it is necessary that we understand holiness.

Holiness and Separateness

When the Bible speaks of God as holy, it is referring first of all to his separateness. God is totally independent of everything he has created. He is unique—he depends upon nothing. As Louis Berkhof puts it, "In its original sense it [God's holiness] denotes that He is absolutely distinct from all His creatures, and is exalted above them in infinite majesty."

The Bible contrasts holiness with that which is common. Something that is holy doesn't share communality. This is particularly true of God. Because he depends on nothing, he lacks communality with anything but himself. The holy is the unique, the different, and the separate. As R. C. Sproul says in his book, *The Holiness of God*, "When the Bible calls God holy, it means primarily that God is transcendently separate." That is, he is above and beyond us.

The same applies to people and things associated with God. The Old Testament ceremonial law separated holiness and the common in very clear ways:

"You must distinguish between the holy and the common, between the unclean and the clean" (Leviticus 10:10).

Her priests do violence to my law and profane my holy things; they do not distinguish between the holy and the common; they teach that there is no difference between the unclean and the clean; and they shut their eyes to the keeping of my Sabbaths, so that I am profaned among them (Ezekiel 22:26).

They are to teach my people the difference between the holy and the common and show them how to distinguish between the unclean and the clean (Ezekiel 44:23).

Holiness and Fire

One of the best ways to understand what *holy* means is to examine the language associated with holiness in the Bible. For example, holiness is associated with fire. We all know the types of images and ideas that fire brings to our mind: fire purifies; it destroys and changes things completely; it is often frightening and mysterious, while being strangely attractive. In Exodus 3:2 and 5 we read:

There the angel of the LORD appeared to him in flames of fire from within the bush. Moses saw that though the bush was on fire it did not burn up...."Do not come any closer," God said. "Take off your sandals, for the place where you are standing is holy ground."

Similar visions of God's holiness being associated with fire were seen on Mount Sinai. When God appeared in the mountain, there was fire and smoke and thick clouds. Nothing was to ascend the mountain, because God was present there. That is God, the holy God!

In the New Testament, the presence of God was associated with fire on the day of Pentecost. Again the purifying differentness of God was evident on this occasion, as tongues of fire appeared on the disciples (Acts 2:1–13). In Hebrews 12:29 God is described as a "consuming fire." This may be an allusion to Deuteronomy 4:24 and God's appearance on Mount Sinai.

When you think of fire, you get some idea of God's absolute separateness. He is clearly independent of all. Fire separates and fire purifies.

Corollaries of Holiness

The Bible also associates holiness and jealousy. Because God is holy, there is a legitimate jealousy that he exercises.

> Joshua said to the people, "You are not able to serve the LORD. He is a holy God; he is a jealous God. He will not forgive your rebellion and your sins. If you forsake the LORD and serve foreign gods, he will turn and bring disaster on you and make an end of you, after he has been good to you" (Joshua 24:19, 20).

Because God is separate and pure, he will not—in fact, cannot—share his honor with others. If people attempt to make God common and equal to false gods, he will destroy them out of a justified jealousy.

The passage in Joshua also reminds us that holiness and wrath go together. In fact, wrath can even be related to fire. Those who do not acknowledge God's pure separateness must be destroyed. They experience the wrath of God, brought upon them by his holiness.

Awesomeness also accompanies holiness. The Psalms are filled with this notion: "Let them praise your great and awesome name—he is holy" (99:3). "He provided redemption for his people; he ordained his covenant forever—holy and awesome is his name" (111:9).

The holy God is also the remote God. Because of God's separateness, he is unapproachable unless he takes the initiative. Remember the situation in Exodus 3:5, where Moses was warned not to come too close without taking off his shoes, because it was holy ground on which he was standing. The same theme was repeated after the Israelites left Egypt: "The people cannot come up Mount Sinai, because you yourself warned us, 'Put limits around the mountain and set it apart as holy' " (Exodus 19:23).

Holiness and cleanness are also associated. This is seen in the "clean" and "unclean" distinctions made frequently in the dietary laws of the Old Testament. Sanitary facilities were even a required part of the laws of Israel in order to make sure that nothing offensive was ever in God's presence.

The Bible associates God's holiness with majesty. "Who among the gods is like you, O LORD? Who is like you—majestic in holiness, awesome in glory, working wonders?" (Exodus 15:11). We ought not to be surprised that God—who is high, holy and lifted up—would be described as the majestic God. His holiness would naturally lead us to think of him in those terms.

A holy and majestic God is one who would naturally be exalted. And God describes himself in such terms: "For this is what the high and lofty One says—he who lives forever, whose name is holy: 'I live in a high and holy place, but also with him who is contrite and lowly in spirit, to revive the spirit of the lowly and to revive the heart of the contrite' " (Isaiah 57:15).

Holiness and Purity

Not only does holiness make God separate from all his creatures, it also makes him pure. His purity is an aspect of his holiness and separateness, so we must understand that purity does not exhaust the biblical meaning of holiness. Likewise we should be aware that purity is an important and necessary part of being holy.

God's holiness means that he is pure with regard to sin. He is completely separate from sin, he is independent of sin. It has no claim on him; he can destroy it, and will not tolerate it in his presence.

Because God is pure with regard to sin, all of his actions and thoughts are pure. God thinks only holy thoughts, and only carries out holy actions. Everything about the activities of God are pure and altogether righteous.

Holiness and Relationships

God's holiness is illustrated in his relationships with men. The story of Nadab and Abihu in Leviticus 10 reminds us of the consequences of God's holiness. Two sons of Aaron offered unauthorized fire before the Lord. As a result, God struck them dead with fire from heaven. God demonstrated that he cannot tolerate disobedience in persons approaching him in worship. He explains to their father Aaron, "Among those who approach me I will show myself holy; in the sight of all the people I will be honored." It is interesting to note that Aaron accepted God's explanation of God's actions in silent agreement.

A similar situation is described in 1 Chronicles 13. The Israelites were bringing the ark back to Jerusalem, so it was a day of much rejoicing. One of the oxen pulling the cart that carried the ark stumbled. When it did, Uzzah, a Kohathite, reached out his hand to steady the ark. The Bible tells us that God was angry with him and struck him dead.

Many people are bothered by this story: they can't understand why such a thing happened, it seems so innocent to us. We think of Uzzah's act as one of concern for the things of the Lord. That is because we forget what Uzzah surely knew:

"After Aaron and his sons have finished covering the holy furnishings and all the holy articles, and when the camp is ready to move, the Kohathites are to come to do the carrying. But they must not touch the holy things or they will die. The Kohathites are to carry those things that are in the Tent of

Meeting" (Numbers 4:15).

Uzzah surely knew that, because the ark was holy, it was not to be touched. In fact, God had given the direct command that if a Kohathite like Uzzah touched the holy things, he would die. A holy God could do no other. Uzzah was struck dead.

There are other responses recorded in the Scriptures of the way men reacted to the holiness of God, such as the story of the calming of the storm in Mark 4. After Jesus had quieted the wind and the waves, we read that his disciples "were terrified and asked each other, 'Who is this? Even the wind and the waves obey him!' " (4:41). We are not the only ones who are terrified in the presence of the holy; the early disciples of Jesus were, too.

You may recall how Peter responded to the great draft of fish: when he saw it, he fell at Jesus' knees and said, "Go away from me, Lord; I am a sinful man!" (Luke 5:8).

A Holy God and a Holy People

The fact that God is holy, separate from all he created and pure in all his thoughts and actions, requires something of those who are his people. The Bible pointedly tells Christians, people who belong to the holy God, that they must be holy—separated to him from the world. They must pattern their thoughts and acts after his pure thinking and acting. "Just as he who called you is holy, so be holy in all you do; for it is written: 'Be holy, because I am holy' " (1 Peter 1:15).

Holiness in the Presence of God

If we expect to enter into the presence of God, then we must become holy. "Make every effort to live in peace with all men and to be holy; without holiness no one will see the Lord" (Hebrews 12:14).

At such a command, you may feel exactly what Isaiah expressed: " 'Woe to me!' I cried. 'I am ruined! For I am a man of unclean lips, and I live among a people of unclean lips, and my eyes have seen the King, the LORD Almighty' " (6:5). You may even feel that you are at risk being in a church building, where people worship in the presence of God. Well, you should.

Nevertheless, the Bible does not encourage us to avoid the presence of God. On the contrary, it tells us to come before him and to do so with boldness. How can that be? The simple fact is that God makes us holy. He is the only one who can do this, because only he is holy. The picture in Isaiah 6 is one of the most beautiful illustrations of how God makes us holy. "Then one of the seraphs flew to me with a live coal in his hand, which he had taken with tongs from the altar. With it he touched my mouth and said, 'See, this has touched your lips; your guilt is taken away and your sin atoned for' " (Isaiah 6:6, 7).

Isaiah pointed forward to that which has since been accomplished. On the cross, Christ bore our sins—he took the guilt of our transgressions upon himself. He died that we might be holy and righteous before God. We can come into the presence of a holy God without fear because we are holy in Christ Jesus. If we believe in him, then we are pure—we have been set apart from this world and all its corrupting influences. We are neither common nor unclean; we are, as the New Testament says, saints—holy ones—of God.

Responding to God's Holiness

But how can we respond to a holy God who would send his holy Son to redeem for himself a holy people? First of all, by acknowledging God's holiness in the midst of the profane world in which we live. Embrace—don't avoid—the holy God: he has become your God if you trust in the Savior.

Once you have acknowledged God's holiness, you must pursue holiness. That is, you must make every effort to separate yourself from this profane and immoral world. Don't let your mind and soul become polluted by this present evil world. As Timothy had to learn to flee youthful lusts, so too must we learn to separate ourselves from the corrupting influences of the world around us.

And if you pursue holiness, then you will be pursuing God.

He is the only source of true holiness. Pursue him and his righteousness, and follow the example of his holy Son. Make his confession yours: "I have come to do the will of him who sent me." Living according to the will of God is the key to the pursuit of holiness.

Review Questions

1. What are some evidences of the profane age in which we live?
2. What is the original meaning of the word *holy?*
3. What are some of the corollaries of holiness?
4. Why did Nadab and Abihu die?
5. What does the holy God require of his people (1 Peter 1:5)?

Discussion Questions

1. How do you deal with the lack of holiness in this age? Are you satisfied with your actions? How could you do better?
2. Which of the corollaries of holiness do you find frightening? Which encouraging? Explain.
3. How would you explain God's purity to someone who is enamored of twentieth-century cultural values?
4. How do you react to the stories of Nadab and Abihu, and Uzzah? Explain.
5. How can you be sure that you can approach God? Would you have any reason to fear God's presence? What takes away those fears?

God Is Powerful

AMERICANS ARE FASCINATED WITH POWER. When public officials refer to the U.S., it is not odd for them to refer to it as the most powerful nation on earth.

Power plays an important role in American culture. Those who dress for success, for example, wear power suits in order to intimidate those with whom they deal. Political leaders are called "power brokers." Government leaders want to be able to exercise power over the opposition. Many elected leaders aspire to be described as the most powerful politician in Washington, D.C.

Others beside politicians and businessmen prize power. In basketball we have power forwards, in football the power-I formation, the power play in hockey, and in baseball there are power hitters.

Even people who use personal computers like to think of themselves as "power users." Power is almost always a word of approbation. Americans like to be called "powerful"; they like to imagine themselves and their country as possessing power.

Of course, power is a relative idea: something is only powerful in comparison to something else. And power usually indicates the ability to control something—or someone—else.

The Pervasive Evidence of God's Power

When Christians talk about power, they should think first

of all of God's power. The Christian church speaks about God as sovereign, to indicate that he is powerful. Sometimes people speak of God's power in terms of his omnipotence, his all-powerfulness.

If we leaf through the Scriptures, examples of the power of God keep jumping out at us page after page. The Bible uses a variety of ways and circumstances to demonstrate to us that God is powerful. The Scriptural evidence for the power of God is so overwhelming that it is difficult for us to comprehend it all. Nevertheless, we should be ready to acknowledge that God is powerful. "One thing God has spoken, two things have I heard: that you, O God, are strong, and that you, O Lord, are loving" (Psalm 62:11).

Because God is powerful, he has absolute authority over everything, both on the earth and in the heavens. He rules over everything, and everything depends on him.

Power Shown in Creation

The early chapters of Genesis provide one of the clearest examples of God's power—his creating power. "In the beginning God created the heavens and the earth" (Genesis 1:1). If you continue to search through the Scriptures, in book after book you will be reminded of God's power displayed in his act of creation. "'You are worthy, our Lord and God, to receive glory and honor and power, for you created all things, and by your will they were created and have their being'" (Revelation 4:11). From Genesis to Revelation, the Bible clearly and obviously portrays God as an all-powerful Creator.

Nothing continues to exist apart from God. All that *is* depends upon him, for its beginning and for its sustenance.

Categories of Power

One of the ways we can get a better handle on what the Bible means when it talks about the power of God is to look at the various categories the Bible uses to describe God.

Begin with the biblical description of the way God created the world. For example:

> By the word of the LORD were the heavens made, their starry host by the breath of his mouth. He gathers the waters of the sea into jars; he puts the deep into storehouses. Let all the earth fear the LORD; let all the people of the world revere him. For he spoke, and it came to be; he commanded, and it stood firm (Psalm 33:6–9).

The psalmist declared that God is powerful, and portrayed his might in vivid detail. He wove together what he saw of the power God, how he reacted to that power and how others ought to react to this powerful God. God exhibited his powerful character in his creating of the world by the word of his power. The psalmist not only declared the power of God: he called upon God's people to submit to such a powerful God.

All the things that God made cannot be compared to God and his being (Isaiah 40:12ff.). All his creatures are much less than he is, because he has made them. Note that some of the things he has made are obviously great; but creation itself can't be compared to God, because it issues from God's great power.

God describes some aspects of his power when he addresses Job. Note how he talks about his power in terms of things he has created. He asks questions about who can figure out where he keeps such things as the hail and the snow (Job 38:22). No man can do the kind of things that God does.

Power and Providence

God also exhibits his power as he works out his providence. "O great and powerful God, whose name is the LORD Almighty, great are your purposes and mighty are your deeds. Your eyes are open to all the ways of men; you reward everyone according to his conduct and as his deeds deserve" (Jeremiah 32:18, 19). Jeremiah reminds his readers that God cared for his people, and that his care was an exercise of his power.

In a similar manner, remember how Joseph attributed his

care to God's power. "But Joseph said to them, 'Don't be afraid. Am I in the place of God? You intended to harm me, but God intended it for good to accomplish what is now being done, the saving of many lives. So then, don't be afraid. I will provide for you and your children.' And he reassured them and spoke kindly to them" (Genesis 50:19–21). Joseph reminded his brothers that, although they intended evil against him, God caused their sinful acts to work out for the good of Joseph and his brothers as well.

God also exercises his power over the forces of nature. We are often struck by how powerful natural forces are. Think about how you react to hurricanes or earthquakes. Yet the Bible reminds us that God is more powerful than they.

Because God made the world, he can and does use it for his own ends. Whatever he proposes, he can accomplish. By contrast, there are many occasions in life when we become aware of the difference between God's exercise of his might and our meager attempts to use power. For example: I have a power saw with a strong engine. Generally it will cut through a piece of wood quickly and efficiently. But if I twist the saw just a little bit, it will bind. The wood will smoke, and the saw will slow down and come to a stop. I need to exercise power in preestablished ways. But it is not so with God—he can use natural forces to accomplish his purposes. The plagues on Egypt are a clear example of the way he used natural forces to accomplish his plans.

God's Power in the Affairs of People

Not only is God's power evident in the way he exercises control over nature, it is also evident in the way in which he exercises control over man. A good example of that is found in the story of the fulfillment of Nebuchadnezzar's dream (Daniel 4:28ff.). Note in particular the contrast between this mighty king who thought he had such great power, and the power that God himself exercised over king Nebuchadnezzar.

Nebuchadnezzar was the most powerful king in his day.

The people who lived under his rule could think of no clearer example of sovereign power, for he exercised dominion over most of the known world. Yet this great Nebuchadnezzar, powerful as he was, was still subservient to God. When he bragged that he was a great king who sent out his armies to conquer other powerful armies, he was struck down by God. In the end he was a wild man, exiled to the meadows where his fingernails would grow long and he would have to eat grass, until he had learned the hard way that he was under the rule of the mighty God.

The stories about Pharaoh provide similar examples. Here again the most powerful king on earth was no match for the power of God, whether he realized it or not. Pharaoh was simply a player in God's grand drama of redemption. He thought he was keeping the Israelite people under his thumb, but in reality God was building for himself a people. When Pharaoh tried to break the children of Israel, he really forged them into a greater nation. All the while he thought he was exercising great power, but he was really an instrument in the hands of the God, who is almighty.

The story of Job records how God exercised his power even over Satan (Job 1 and 2). The devil had power only to do the things God allowed him to do. He was completely subservient to the Father in heaven.

Power and Redemption

The redemption of the people of God in the Old Testament provides another graphic illustration of God's power. Note, for example, the way in which the Israelites were delivered from the hand of Pharaoh. The Israelites were weak; they had no power whatsoever on their own. Yet they walked away from their oppressors unscathed.

Some of the incidents that accompanied their deliverance bewilder modern scientific people. The Israelites were commanded to put the blood of the Passover lamb on their door posts. Twentieth-century people can't figure out how such an act could accomplish anything. But because this was an act of faith, of confidence in the power of God, when the angel of death came to Egypt he passed over the homes of the Israelites. In contrast the Egyptians, who seemed to be so powerful, sustained the death of the firstborn in each of their households.

The contrast continued when the Israelites arrived at the Red Sea. Here was a hopeless situation: the water blocked them in front, and Pharaoh's army stood poised to attack them from behind. From all appearances, it was a hopeless, helpless situation. But God exercised his power: he opened the sea, and the Israelites crossed on dry land. When Pharaoh and his hosts attempted to follow close behind, they were swallowed up in the sea as the power of God caused it to return to its course. The mighty army of Pharaoh was no match for God; what a demonstration of his might!

Over and over again, the events of the exodus journey recall God's power. He provided fresh manna daily, water from rocks, and victory over mighty enemies. All of this was a part of the powerful way that God redeemed his people.

The Clearest Example of God's Power

The clearest manifestation of God's power is shown in the work of Jesus Christ. Jesus did not accomplish redemption in the way most people expected him to—he didn't demonstrate his authority according to the norms of this world. Even his own disciples were expecting him to do something different, dramatic and exciting. Instead, Jesus came into the world meek and lowly. His death was ignominious, lowly and insignificant. But he established a kingdom that will last forever.

The crowning display of God's power in redemption is Jesus' resurrection from the dead. After his crucifixion, of course, Jesus was dead: his heart had stopped and no blood was pumping through him. Yet, three days after his death, God raised him from the dead. Neither modern powers of any sort nor the most highly advanced medical science could come close to doing anything like that. Only the power of God could have raised Jesus from the grave!

Attempts to Avoid God's Power

Sometimes when we think about God's power, certain questions are raised in our minds. Some of them are trivial, others are significant.

There are those who foolishly imagine that they can relieve themselves of the fear of God, the all-powerful, by figuring out ways to make his power seem inconsequential. For example: Skeptics ask, Is God powerful enough to make a rock that he could not pick up? When dealing with frivolous questions like this, we need to remember that God's infinite power cannot be isolated from his other attributes, but is exercised in consort with all his other characteristics, such as wisdom, love and goodness. He wouldn't stoop to use his power to satisfy the idle curiosity of sinful men.

God's Power and His Other Attributes

We must acknowledge that there are some things that God cannot do. He cannot be something other than God. The Bible tells us that he cannot deny himself.

Because God is just, he can never be unfair; being good, he couldn't possibly do anything evil; since he is wise, foolishness would be unthinkable in him. His power is only a single element in the fullness of his character—it could never be isolated from the rest.

The Bible seldom describes God's power in abstraction. It is almost always described in terms of its relationship to his creation or to his people:

Come and see what God has done, how awesome his works in man's behalf! He turned the sea into dry land, they passed through the water on foot—come, let us rejoice in him. He rules forever by his power, his eyes watch the nations—let not the rebellious rise up against him (Psalm 66:5–7).

God's Power and Our Worship

There are a number of things that an understanding of the power of God ought to do for us. When we reflect on his might, we ought to experience a sense of awe. "I have seen you in the sanctuary and beheld your power and your glory. Because your love is better than life, my lips will glorify you" (Psalm 63:2).

Many twentieth-century men have difficulty experiencing awe. Many of us are a little bit skeptical of anything we would describe as awe-inspiring. But the contemplation of God's power ought to catch us up short. When we reflect upon it, we should have the same kind of response that we do when we look over the edge of a high cliff or building. Our breath ought to become short and difficult, because God's power is so awesome.

We also ought to see that God's power can help us as we come into his presence for worship. In this modern world, we don't have many analogies to coming into the presence of a great king. But we can't help remembering the way Esther came before King Xerxes. She was safe only if he let her stay alive. Kings operate that way, and so does God.

God is much more powerful than any mortal king, and when we come into his presence, it ought to be with a sense of fear as well as anticipation. But the fact of the matter is that this mighty God is one who invites us into his presence, before the very throne of grace—and to come with boldness, through the blood of Jesus Christ.

The worship of God should be something we look forward to. We ought to rejoice in the opportunity to experience and express our response to the almighty One. There are numerous songs and hymns that rejoice in his might, and they can help us

GOD IS POWERFUL

to express our awe in the presence of such a great and powerful God. It would be appropriate, then, to say that the power
constrains us to worship him.

God's Power and Our Weakness

A better understanding of God's power ought to help us
overcome our own cowardice and weakness. Such strength is
available to all who trust in him. He doesn't just show off his
power—he shares it with his people.

Just before his ascension, Jesus spoke of this when he said,
"All authority in heaven and earth has been given to me"
(Matthew 28:18). And then he reminded his disciples—and
us—that he is with us always. We should conclude that God's
power is available to us in carrying out the commission Christ
has given to his church.

Note how this power was evident in the lives of the disciples. After Christ's resurrection, they went out and preached
the gospel. And they did it with such vigor that they were
described as turning the world upside down!

Power and Obedience

The power of God also helps us to overcome our fears. If
God's power is available to us and encourages us, then we
shouldn't be afraid of anything. No matter how powerful those
opposing us may be, we know that God is stronger. Therefore
we ought to be encouraged to testify about—and to render
faithful service to—our wonderful Savior.

God's power should also encourage us in our ordinary
living. Many of us know what we should do and are committed
to doing it, but we don't feel that we can. We profess to be
unable, to lack the power, to do what God calls upon us to do.
We claim it's too hard for us.

The Bible tells us that we don't have things because we don't
ask for them. If we ask God, then we will have them. When we
think about all the things we know we have to do, and then think

about God's power, we ought to be able to go about doing what he commands.

Power and Confidence

Our understanding of the power of God ought to give us a great deal of comfort. It is an amazing power, and we can rest securely upon it. Look how Paul wrote to the church of Rome: he talked about God's amazing power, and asked the rhetorical question, If God is for us, who can be against us? It's not that Christ's church had no enemies; they were legion, and very active. But not one of them could stand against such a mighty God. All the powers that Paul listed at the end of Romans 8 are insignificant in comparison to the power of our sovereign Lord.

As Christians, we must remind ourselves that God makes his strength available to us. He binds himself to us in what the Bible calls a covenant. It's as though God had written a contract and signed his name to it—a contract that says, "I will look after you and use my power to protect, encourage and comfort you."

Our God demonstrated his commitment to that contract by sending his own Son to die in our place. It's as though that contract were written in the blood of our Lord Jesus Christ.

Reflecting on the power of God ought to lead us to love and serve him more courageously. He has promised in his covenant that he will watch over us, to exercise his power on our behalf. With that assurance, we should be able to serve him without any thought of the risks. If God is for us and uses his might on our behalf, then surely we cannot fail. He is powerful, and we can serve him with power, because he works in and through us.

Review Questions

1. How does God show his power in creation?
2. How does God show his power in providence?
3. Contrast God's power with that of Pharaoh and Nebuchadnezzar.
4. How do people attempt to deny God's power?

5. How does God show his power in redemption?

Discussion Questions

1. Describe the effect God's power should have on you as you worship.
2. How can you use the Bible's teaching about God's power to encourage you to obey him?
3. What aspect of God's power do you find most helpful?
4. Have you experienced God's power in your life? Explain.
5. How can you use the stories of God's power found in the Bible to help you live as a Christian today?

God Is Good

God is great. God is good.
And we thank him for our food.

MANY OF US HAVE LEARNED THIS PRAYER as little children, and often said it before meals. You probably didn't think much about it—other than that the poem did not quite rhyme.

Nevertheless, the poem does contain an important idea that all Christians need to keep in mind—that God is good. If we ever forget this, then we have lost one of his most significant attributes. For not only does it explain why we are fed, but in his goodness he provides us with many additional benefits.

Goodness, like so many of the attributes of God, is both simple and profound. It is simple in that any small child can appreciate, in his own way, that God is good. The thought of God's goodness is profound because it encompasses many sophisticated theological ideas.

J. I. Packer defines good as follows:

> Good in Scripture is not an abstract quality, nor is it a secular human ideal; "good" means first and foremost what God is...then what He does, creates, commands, and gives, and finally what He approves in the lives of His creatures (New Bible Dictionary).

Goodness is one attribute that characterizes God. Therefore, if we are going to describe God, it makes sense that we do so in terms of his goodness.

True Goodness Is Found Only in God

As with so many of the other positive things in this world, true and absolute goodness is found only in God. All other goodness is derived from him and his goodness.

We must be careful that we don't water down what the Bible says about God's goodness. He alone can make something good—Jesus himself further elaborated on this theme in his conversation with the rich young ruler: "As Jesus started on his way, a man ran up to him and fell on his knees before him. 'Good teacher', he asked, 'what must I do to inherit eternal life?' 'Why do you call me good?' Jesus answered. 'No one is good—except God alone' " (Mark 10:17). Jesus used the fact that God is good, and the assurance that people knew this, to establish important theological truths about himself. The reason he can be good is because he himself is God.

Goodness Conforms to God's Standards

Since God is the source of all goodness, it stands to reason that anything described as good would conform to his standards. For goodness not to accord with God's practical, moral and religious attributes would not be fitting—it would be like a surgeon showing up for his wedding still dressed in his surgical garb. There is nothing wrong with it in the operating room, but it would be inappropriate in a wedding, with the bride in her formal gown. So it is with goodness: it should fit in with the other characteristics of God.

We see the appropriateness of God's nature and goodness in the way the work of the Holy Spirit is described as good. It would be impossible for God the Spirit to lead in anything but a good way, so the psalmist describes the Holy Spirit as good. "Teach me to do your will, for you are my God; may your good Spirit lead me on level ground" (Psalm 143:10).

In a similar way, the work that God does in his people is characterized as good. The Holy Spirit bears fruit in the lives of his people, and that fruit is described as good. "The fruit of the Spirit is...goodness" (Galatians 5:22).

God's Goodness in Israel's History

Think of any historical setting. When a formative influence is present, it comes to characterize much of what it touches. For example, one of the greatest influences on the history of English-speaking people was the Norman conquest of England in 1066. When the Normans invaded, they imposed their language, which was based on Latin, on the English. As a result, a great portion of English vocabulary is derived from Latin.

I know a teacher of Latin who knew how much English had been influenced by Latin, and he used that knowledge as a motivational tool for his students. He offered a point on his tests for any student who could stump him on the meaning of any English word. If the word was derived from Latin, he would show the students how useful the study of Latin was in using their native tongue. He was able to demonstrate the influence of Latin on the language by this clever device.

Just as Latin words are found throughout the English language, so is evidence of God's goodness seen in history— particularly that of his people Israel. Because God was active in forming and developing Israel, his goodness was evident in all aspects of their history. It couldn't be any other way. God's goodness includes what God does.

For example, God demonstrated his goodness to Israel when he brought them out of Egypt. It wasn't simply a leading out, but a dramatic rescue from Pharaoh's army. Moses' father-in-law indicated that what the Lord did in delivering the Israelites was a good thing. "Jethro was delighted to hear about all the good things the LORD had done for Israel in rescuing them from the hand of the Egyptians" (Exodus 18:9).

Goodness and Forgiveness

Another constant in Israel's life was sin. As a people and as individuals, they rebelled against God and broke his law, and God regularly forgave them. Why did God do this? Hezekiah says that God forgave sin because he is good. "But Hezekiah prayed for them, saying, 'May the LORD, who is good, pardon everyone who sets his heart on seeking God—the LORD, the God of his fathers' " (2 Chronicles 30:18).

Not only should we recognize that God is good when he forgives lawbreakers, we should remember also that the law of God itself is good. Both the Old Testament and the New argue that God's law is good:

> Take away the disgrace I dread, for your laws are good (Psalm 119:39).

> So then, the law is holy, and the commandment is holy, righteous and good (Romans 7:12).

And if God's law is good, then his will is also good. That is what Paul assumes when he states that "you will be able to test and approve what God's will is—his good, pleasing and perfect will" (Romans 12:2).

We shouldn't be surprised that the Bible describes both the law of God and the will of God as good. How else could something that reflects the character and nature of God be described? If God is good, then what he requires and what he desires will of necessity be good.

The Character of God's Goodness

Goodness belongs to God. He and he alone is good. But what is the nature and character of God's goodness?

This attribute of God is sometimes called "lovingkindness," a particularly important Old Testament concept. Lovingkindness is closely connected with two similar ideas. The first is that of covenant. God relates to his people in terms of a covenant—a solemn bond between God and his people. His dealings with his people in this special relationship are best characterized by the idea of lovingkindness.

A second and closely allied aspect of lovingkindness is

faithfulness. In God's covenantal relationships with his people, they can be assured that he will be reliable. The essence of the covenantal bond is that God can be counted on to keep his promises.

The New Bible Dictionary defines lovingkindness (based on the Hebrew word *hesed*) as "steadfast love on the basis of a covenant." The psalmist pictures this steadfast love in Psalm 89, where God says,

> I will not take my love from him, nor will I ever betray my faithfulness. I will not violate my covenant or alter what my lips have uttered. Once for all, I have sworn by my holiness—and I will not lie to David—that his line will continue forever and his throne endure before like the sun (verses 33–36).

Goodness as Grace

God's goodness is sometimes seen as grace, his unmerited favor toward his people. It is not earned, nor is it ever a reward to God's people. It is solely and exclusively an evidence of God's goodness.

All have sinned, all deserve God's wrath and curse. But grace is God's unmerited favor, which leads to the salvation of a great host of guilty sinners. Again, an evidence of the fact that God is good.

Goodness in Creation

Everything that God has made reflects his goodness. For example: when he had completed his work of creation, God declared that all that he had made was good. "God saw all that he had made, and it was very good" (Genesis 1:31).

Just as everything God made is good, so too is everything he gives us. In fact, anything we have that is good came from God. "Every good and perfect gift is from above, coming down from the Father of the heavenly lights, who does not change like shifting shadows" (James 1:17).

There are some things that come into our lives that we refuse to regard as good. For example, there are plenty of women who, when they discover they are pregnant, think—and their husbands agree—that a disaster has struck. They regard bearing and caring for another child as a burden or a distasteful obligation. Yet later on, they often realize that the child was indeed a gift from God, and wonderfully good.

Goodness Leads to Praise

God's goodness should lead us to give praise and thanksgiving to him for his goodness. No other response makes any sense. "Give thanks to the LORD, for he is good: his love endures forever" (1 Chronicles 16:34).

Anyone who does not respond to God with praise and thanksgiving for his goodness is like someone who takes a book to a football game to read. As touchdowns are scored, as fans shout and encourage their favorite team, such a one simply continues his reading. You would say, "Why didn't he just stay at home and read? What a fool!" So too is anyone who does not experience joy and gratitude for the goodness of the Lord.

The Withdrawal of God's Goodness

There are those who complain that they can see no evidence of the goodness of God in their lives. Many who say such things are clearly mistaken; for while they are complaining they are eating their food, living in nice houses and wearing fine clothes. Others, of course, may not be so richly blessed; but even they are indebted to God for whatever they do have.

If we serve other gods, we cannot expect to receive good from the Lord. Joshua once said to Israel, "If you forsake the LORD and serve foreign gods, he will turn and bring disaster on you and make an end of you, after he has been good to you" (Joshua 24:20). This was frequently the case with the Israelites— Joshua's prediction came true over and over again.

Often, however, the withholding of God's blessing was

merely temporary. He was really being kind to his people—he was bringing calamity upon them only to remind them that they were not to follow false gods. And so, what at first seemed to be evidence of the loss of God's favor was really his way of showing them his goodness.

Goodness Cannot Be Earned

No one has a claim on God's goodness; it is not something that we can earn. God does not need to be good to his people. Nevertheless, he does tell us that he will be good to certain people, and he even tells us why that is the case.

For example, those who follow God faithfully are assured that he will be faithful to them and bless them. All who are pure in heart have received such a promise from him: "Surely God is good to Israel, to those who are pure in heart" (Psalm 73:1).

"You are my Lord; apart from you I have no good thing" (Psalm 16:2). This confession of the psalmist is one that we must learn to make regularly. All the good we have has come from God, and he will continue to sustain us, whether in triumph or in tragedy. He will bring to fruition all those of our desires that reflect his goodness. He will be with all who are pure in heart.

As the pure in heart, we can expect to survive and prosper in the years to come because of God's goodness. We would do well to resolve continually to acknowledge and be grateful to him as his mercies fall upon us.

Response to God's Goodness

The recipients of God's goodness are called upon to respond to the God of goodness. The psalmist reminds the people of God to express gratitude to him for his lovingkindness. "Give thanks to the LORD, for he is good" (Psalm 136:1).

This attitude is pictured in the book of Hosea. There the people of God are called upon to exhibit steadfast love for him. Anything less is graphically depicted as spiritual adultery.

As those who benefit from God's goodness, we should be

filled with a deep desire to love and serve him. Because God is good, he deserves our loving service. Moreover, because God is good to us, we are all the more obligated to serve *him*. Loving and serving a God who is good should never be seen as a burden or an onerous duty. Rather, it should burst unrestrained from those who are beneficiaries of his lovingkindness.

Loving and serving God leads us to love and serve others. His people are expected to treat others kindly. In fact, Jesus tells us that if we love him, we will do what he commands. As we have opportunity, the Savior and head of the church wants us to "do good to all people, especially to those who belong to the family of believers" (Galatians 6:10).

In a specific way, we can love God—and also be serving him—when we gently restore one who is caught in sin (Galatians 6:1), Sinners who have been forgiven because of God's goodness should be ready to receive a brother or sister in the Lord who has sinned against them, and not hold grudges or withhold forgiveness.

Sometimes you may feel that you have been stretched to the limit in helping others. When you feel that way, think of what God in his goodness has done for *you*. Reminding yourself of how good God has been to you should enable you to love and serve him more effectively. "Let us not become weary in doing good, for at the proper time we will reap a harvest if we do not give up" (Galatians 6:9).

Remember: The harvest comes from God, who demonstrates his goodness in all he does, makes, says, and gives. With that in mind, be good because God is good.

Review Questions

1. How does Jesus use the idea that only God is good to support his claims to be divine (see Mark 10)?
2. How is God's goodness associated with his lovingkindness?
3. What is the relationship between God's goodness and his grace?
4. How does creation reflect God's goodness?
5. List some of the benefits of God's goodness.

Discussion Questions

1. Which manifestations of God's goodness do you find most beneficial? Explain.
2. What reactions do you have when you think of God's goodness? How would you like to change them?
3. Do you ever feel that you don't benefit from God's goodness? What is the antidote for such feelings?
4. How will you use the Bible's teaching about God's goodness to love him more and serve him better?
5. Why is praise such a fitting response to God's goodness? Do you always respond to his goodness by praising him? If not, how can you change?

God Is Wise

Nﾍ ONE OF US WANTS TO BE THOUGHT OF AS A FOOL, and most of us would take offense if someone went around calling us one.

On the other hand, few of us self-consciously desire to be wise. Rather, we would like to be thought of as intelligent, informed, brilliant, erudite, maybe wealthy, perhaps even respected. But seldom do we see being a fool as the opposite of being wise.

The Scriptures make it clear, however, that wisdom is something to be prized. It is to be prized because God himself is described for us in the Bible as wise, as the all-wise One—indeed, as the source of all wisdom.

God Is Wise in All He Does

The Bible is clear when it speaks of God's wisdom. Wisdom belongs to God's essence, is a part of his essential character. To think about God one must think of him as wise.

In many places, the Old Testament reminds us that he is wise. Job 12:13 says, "To God belong wisdom and power, counsel and understanding are his." Daniel repeats the same refrain: "Praise be to the name of God for ever and ever; wisdom and power are his" (2:20).

The New Testament makes the same point. In the last book

of the Bible, the apostle John says that the Son, as well as the Father, are characterized by wisdom. "Worthy is the Lamb, who was slain, to receive power and wealth and wisdom and strength and honor and glory and praise!" (Revelation 5:12). Likewise John records that the church responds, "Amen! Praise and glory and wisdom and thanks and honor and power and strength be to our God for ever and ever. Amen!" (7:12).

When we think of certain people, we are likely to recall certain of their characteristics. For instance: when I think about my friend Roy, I think about a delightful sense of humor. All who know him do—humor is a part of Roy. That is why he is always being asked to serve as master of ceremonies at various functions. He has a story for every occasion. It is almost impossible to think about him without recalling his incredibly good sense of humor.

One of my closest friends is remembered as being neat and organized. As a seminary classmate of his, I recollect that his notes were always in perfect shape. He never had a page out of place or a curled edge on a sheet of notepaper. That's the kind of person he is: neatness characterizes him.

In the same way, when we think about God we ought to remember his wisdom—an essential characteristic that he possesses beyond measure. And when we think of wisdom as belonging to God's essence, we are reminded that it covers all aspects of God, it cuts across everything about God.

Curiosity is my specialty—I'm just inquisitive about things. Oftentimes, just discovering things is much more important to me than doing things. When I was preparing to move to Mississippi I got rid of a lot of things, including many folders in my files. As I went through them, I found a fat folder containing all sorts of information on—of all things—wood stoves. I had gotten interested in them a number of years ago. I collected all types of information on the stoves and their operation, and studied it all. Once I had done all this, installing my own was anticlimactic. Having it around wasn't something that was very important to me, but finding out about it was.

An insatiable curiosity has characterized almost all aspects of my life. When I don't know something, I am driven to find out about it. Just as curiosity characterizes almost everything I do, so God's wisdom characterizes everything he does. It operates in all his actions.

The way that God's wisdom characterizes him is similar to the way in which some people think about dessert. If I say "dessert" to some people, they will think "chocolate." They may be able to conceive of the notion of vanilla wafers or rice pudding being construed as dessert; but dessert is *really* chocolate. It is *always* chocolate—that's what dessert *is*. And so it is with God: he is always wise. Again, everything about him is characterized by his wisdom. He is wise in everything.

I have another significant characteristic: poor vision. Everything I do is influenced by my inability to see clearly. The first thing I do in the morning is to put on my glasses so that I can get to the bathroom and put in my contact lenses. Work and play are constantly governed by whether I have on my glasses or my contacts. Equally certain is it that God is always wise. Once more: everything he does is characterized by his wisdom.

But we need to know more about this characteristic that we ought to see in God over and over again.

What Is Wisdom?

Wisdom, as it is portrayed for us in the Scriptures, has to do with accomplishment—with getting things done, with bringing things to a certain end. It has to do with accomplishing ends in the most effective way possible. Wisdom includes the ideas of cleverness and efficiency. These are all built into someone who is wise.

But above all, this ability to get things done, and understanding how to do things, is formed by moral understanding—a commitment to doing things in the way that is right, proper and just. The wise person does things in a way that brings honor to the God who has made the whole world.

These characteristics of wisdom, as they are presented to us in the Scriptures, demonstrate how appropriate it is for us to think about God as being all-wise.

Wisdom has to do with making choices, deciding things, and exercising skills, abilities and talents in a very special way. It is easy to see how these things are related to God.

Wisdom and Knowledge

God's wisdom and knowledge relate to one another. He knows everything, he's never baffled by anything, his wisdom is unbounded. Nor is he ever confused by some new idea or bit of information that he needs to study so that he can make a better decision or accomplish something more effectively.

Because God is never mistaken, his wisdom is never corrupted. He never comes to a wrong conclusion. He is never constrained because there's something he's unable to consider, or something he hasn't thought about.

Wisdom and Righteousness

God's wisdom is also informed by his righteousness. And so God—because he is the all-righteous God, because he doesn't think evil thoughts, because he is wise—always does things correctly, properly.

It's not easy to understand the relationship between God's righteousness and his wisdom. Since we are not wise or righteous like God, we will never be able to do things—never be able to think things—without once crossing over the line into error. But God, because he is righteous, can do things we cannot.

The Scriptures see God and man in sharp contrast. Man tries to do things wisely, but evil interferes and twists, perverts and thwarts his attempts. Isaiah warns,

Woe to those who go down to Egypt for help, who rely on horses, who trust in the multitude of their chariots and in the great strength of their horsemen, but do not look to the Holy One of Israel, or seek help from the LORD. Yet he too is wise and can bring disaster; he does not take back his words. He will rise up against the house of the wicked, against those who help evildoers (31:1, 2).

"You may go look for wisdom someplace else," Isaiah is saying. "You may even go to those who earn their living as wise men. But their wisdom is nothing like the wisdom of God." Whatever our God does is right and just. And that's another characteristic of his wisdom.

God, the Only Source of Wisdom

The Bible also tells us that if we want to find wisdom, we must seek it in God, the only source. The writer of Proverbs says, "For the LORD gives wisdom, and from his mouth come knowledge and understanding" (2:6). There is no wisdom in this world that can be compared with God's wisdom—none whatsoever. God's wisdom is his alone.

In fact, Jeremiah had a good way to characterize the difference between the wisdom of God and foolishness of this world:

> No one is like you, O LORD; you are great, and your name is mighty in power. Who should not revere you, O King of the nations? This is your due. Among all of the wise men of the nations and in all their kingdoms, there is no one like you. They are all senseless and foolish; they are taught by worthless wooden idols. Hammered silver is brought from Tarshish and gold from Uphaz. What the craftsman and goldsmith have made is then dressed in blue and purple—all made by skilled workers. But the LORD is the true God; he is the living God, the eternal King. When he is angry, the earth trembles; the nations cannot endure his wrath. "Tell them this: 'These gods, who did not make the heavens and the earth, will perish from the earth and from under the heavens.' " But God made the earth by his power; he founded the world by his wisdom and stretched out the heavens by his understanding (Jeremiah 10:6–12).

God's Wisdom and Worldly Wisdom

The Scriptures clearly assert that any wisdom apart from

God's is counterfeit. God, and God alone, is the one source of all wisdom. In fact there is a striking contrast: what the world thinks is wise turns out to be total foolishness.

The first chapter of 1 Corinthians develops this same Old Testament theme. The apostle Paul claims that God shows the wisdom of this world to be foolishness. As a matter of fact, Paul says that the things this world calls foolishness—including the "foolishness" of the cross—God used to save his people. In his wisdom, he made a way in which people could come to a state of eternal bliss, into a state of salvation through the Redeemer, Jesus Christ.

God is all-wise. His wisdom characterizes all his thoughts and actions. Therefore, when Christians think about God they should think about him as the only wise God.

Evidence of God's Wisdom in Creation

The Scriptures portray God's wisdom as marvelous and unique. The Bible also gives us evidence that God really is a wise God. One of the most obvious ways in which Scripture does this is by describing his role in creation, where we see clear evidences of his wisdom. "How many are your works, O LORD. In wisdom you made them all. The earth is full of your creatures" (Psalm 104:24).

The bulk of Psalm 104 shows God's wisdom in creation:

He set the earth on its foundations; it can never be moved. You covered it with the deep as with a garment; the waters stood above the mountains. At your rebuke the waters fled. At the sound of your thunder they took flight; they flowed over the mountains, they went down into the valleys, to the place you assigned for them. You set a boundary they cannot cross; never again will they trouble the earth. He makes springs pour water into the ravines; it flows between the mountains. They give water to all of the beasts of the fields (5–10).

The way in which God created the waters and how he made them function demonstrate that he is wise: "There is the sea, vast and spacious, teeming with creatures beyond number—living things both large and small. Here the ships go to and fro and the leviathan, which you formed to frolic there" (Psalm 104:25, 26).

God's design for creation is further evidence of his wisdom. The provisions and relationships that prevail in the created order could be brought into being only by a wise God:

> The birds of the air nest by the waters; they sing among the branches. He waters the mountains from his upper chambers; the earth is satisfied by the fruit of his work. He makes grass grow for cattle, and makes plants for man to cultivate—bringing forth food from the earth: wine that gladdens the heart of man, oil to make his face shine, and bread that sustains his heart. The trees of the LORD are well watered, the cedars of Lebanon that he planted. There the birds make their nests; the stork has its home in the pine trees. The high mountains belong to the wild goats; the crags are a refuge for the coneys (Psalm 104:12–18).

The psalmist describes the way God caused the sun and the moon to set off the seasons, making it possible for night creatures to crawl about and "seek their food from God" (Psalm 104:21). When the sun rises, man "goes out to his work, to his labor until evening" (104:23). The writer, in setting forth all these different aspects of creation, display God's wisdom. "How many are your works, O LORD! In wisdom you made them all" (104:24).

When we look at the world around us and see all the marvels of God's creation, we should recognize that only a wise God—who does everything in the most effective way possible—could build an orderly, magnificent world such as this.

Evidences of God's Wisdom in Providence

The Bible not only points to creation for evidence of God's wisdom; it also directs our attention to God's works of providence to find more evidence that God is wise: "The LORD foils the plans of the nations; he thwarts the purposes of the peoples.

But the plans of the LORD stand firm forever, the purposes of his heart through all generations" (Psalm 33:10, 11).

As the ancient Hebrews sang this song, don't you think they thought about how God spoiled the plans of the evil ones, those who are his enemies, and how he brought about his own plans? They would recall how he rescued the Israelites, a lowly, poor group of slaves living in Egypt; and how he was able to thwart the plans of Pharaoh, who tried to keep them in Egypt. Despite having the most sophisticated weapons of war, Pharaoh was unable to recapture these poor slaves.

From a military point of view, Pharaoh could not have been in a better position. There was water in front of the Israelites, and Pharaoh with all his chariots behind them. But God thwarted the plans of Pharaoh: instead of recapturing his runaway slaves, Pharaoh along with his armies were drowned in the sea while the Israelites escaped on dry land.

The evidences of God's wisdom in overcoming Pharaoh are repeated over and over again in the history of the Israelites. Think of what happened to the Amalekites, who would not let the Israelites go their way, or how God thwarted the plans of Barak, king of Moab, when he brought Balaam to curse the Israelites. Follow the chain of events recorded in Exodus, and you can see the awesome ways in which God's wisdom is exhibited in the providential preservation of his people.

The New Testament rehearses the same theme of God's wisdom as shown in his providence:

> And we know that in all things God works for the good of those who love him, who have been called according to his purpose....For I am convinced that neither death nor life, neither angels nor demons, neither the present nor the future, nor any powers, neither height nor depth, nor anything else in all creation, will be able to separate us from the love of God that is in Christ Jesus our Lord (Romans 8:28, 38, 39).

The apostle Paul was sounding the same theme as the ancient psalmist: God can thwart the plans of his enemies, but nothing can upset his own designs (cf. Psalm 33:10). Clearly, nothing can frustrate his plans, because they are devised by the all-wise One.

Evidences of God's Wisdom in Redemption

Just as creation and providence are filled with evidences of God's wisdom, so also is his work of redemption. Paul, after describing God's great plan of salvation in the first few chapters of Romans, goes off into a great doxology: "Oh, the depth of the riches of the wisdom and knowledge of God! How unsearchable his judgments, and his paths beyond tracing out!" (Romans 11:33). Paul is mindful of the marvel of God's wisdom in designing his plan of salvation, a plan that brought together Jew and Gentile, a plan that allowed God to be both just and the justifier of his sinful people.

When Paul wrote to the church at Corinth, he reminded them of God's wisdom in redemption: "For the message of the cross is foolishness to those who are perishing, but to us who are being saved it is the power of God. For it is written: 'I will destroy the wisdom of the wise; the intelligence of the intelligent I will frustrate.' " (1 Corinthians 1:18, 19).

The world calls the cross foolishness; but in the hands of a wise God it is an instrument of the triumph of wisdom.

Evidence of God's Wisdom in the Church

It's not just in the things that God has made, it's not just in God's preserving all of his people, it's not just in the plan of salvation that we see the marvels of God's wisdom. "His intent was that now, through the church, the manifold wisdom of God should be made known to the rulers and authorities in the heavenly realms, according to his eternal purpose which he accomplished in Christ Jesus our Lord" (Ephesians 3:10, 11).

It was in the church where these two different peoples—the Jew and the Gentile—got together. There we see the manifold wisdom of God. We see the wisdom of God as the church of Jesus Christ functions in the way in which God designed it.

The church shows God's wisdom as it becomes a healthy and healing community. Because of the wisdom of God, the church accepts people, shows them the love of Christ, encourages them when downcast. In an earlier chapter of this book, I told of an incident when my wife was ill. The congregation of which we were a part demonstrated how the manifold wisdom of God is shown in the church. I can well remember during my wife's illness how the doorbell would ring, I would answer the door, and a member of the congregation would greet me by saying, "I know how hard it is. Can I clean the kitchen for you?" You see, that is God's wisdom.

As the church of Jesus Christ does the things that the church is supposed to do, we see the wisdom of God. The church should encourage people in the service of the Lord by giving people opportunities to teach, to counsel one another, to engage in the works of service that the apostle Paul says all of us should carry out (Ephesians 4:12).

And so it is in the midst of the church of Jesus Christ that we see the wisdom of God being demonstrated in all of these ways. The church differs from the world. In the great church of Jesus Christ, the fellowship of the redeemed, we know that we can have constant encouragement and blessing, because the church reflects God's many-sided wisdom.

Responding to God's Wisdom

Look around you, and you will see in creation evidences of an all-wise God. Reflect on how God saved his people and preserved them throughout history, and you will see clearly that God is wise. As you function in the church of Jesus Christ—as you minister and are ministered to—you will be convinced that God is an all-wise God.

His Word tells us that God is wise. It instructs us in the character of his wisdom and reminds us of the overwhelming evidence that God is wise. That Word also calls us to be wise. Wisdom, according to the Bible, begins by fearing God: "The fear of the LORD is the beginning of wisdom, and knowledge of the Holy One is understanding" (Proverbs 9:10).

One of the most sensible things that Christians can do is to fear God, to submit humbly to the Savior. In so doing, you respond appropriately to the Bible's teaching about the wisdom of God. You will be able to incorporate into your life the evidence of his wisdom all around you. Just as wisdom befits a God like ours, so wisdom befits the people of such a God.

Perhaps more than any other, the apostle John provides the vehicle for our response:

> "Worthy is the Lamb, who was slain, to receive power and wealth and wisdom and strength and honor and glory and praise!" Then I heard every creature in heaven and on earth and under the earth and on the sea, and all that is in them, singing: "To him who sits on the throne and to the Lamb be praise and honor and glory and power, for ever and ever!" The four living creatures said, "Amen," and the elders fell down and worshiped (Revelation 5:12–14).

Wise people join with the heavenly hosts and praise God for his wisdom. Wise people worship the wise God.

God in his wisdom has provided the church as a place where his people can love him and serve him. Wise people respond to God's beneficence by engaging in loving service.

Review Questions

1. How does Psalm 104 show that God is wise?
2. In what way does Paul contrast the wisdom of God with the wisdom of the world?
3. Where does the Bible say that wisdom begins? Describe that starting point.
4. How is God's wisdom shown in redemption?
5. How does the church make known God's manifold wisdom?

Discussion Questions

1. How would you defend yourself against the charge that Christians are naive, foolish people?
2. What do you think is the most convincing evidence that God is wise? Explain.

3. When you look at your congregation, do you see evidences of God's wisdom? How could the congregation change in order to show his wisdom more clearly?
4. Do you think of yourself as wise? Why or why not? How could you acquire more wisdom?
5. What is the relationship between loving and serving God and being a wise person?

Loving and Serving God

T HE FIRST CHAPTER OF THIS BOOK began with a description of
an incident that occurred at the end of a trip. It is appropriate,
then, for the book to end with a reflection on the journey that
you, the reader, have been taking. For indeed, this book was a
journey through the Bible, looking at various aspects of God's
character.

No doubt there were many topics that you wanted to
examine in more detail, but the time was short or the subject too
detailed. But just as a trip introduces one to many things to see
on another visit, so this book should encourage you to return to
study those matters again.

There are other topics that were not covered. As with any
trip, there are probably many things you would like to see that
were not included. If you experienced some of these feelings,
then this book has accomplished one of its purposes—namely,
to introduce people to some aspects of the doctrine of God with
the hope that they would continue in their investigation.

What Happens When You Study about God

But a study about God should do more than whet our
appetite for a deeper, fuller examination of the subject. Such an
exercise should lead God's people to experience changes in

their lives. The changes this book sought to bring about revolve around the necessity for the people of God to love and serve him. As has frequently been pointed out in this book, God deserves to be loved and served by his children, because of who he is and what he has done.

Throughout, hints have been given as to how one can better love and serve God. One of the primary focal points is that, as we get to know God, we will be more desirous of loving him and therefore will be more adept at serving him.

How to Know God

To love God requires that we know who God is. The Bible warns that there is a danger that people will worship the vain imaginations of their own hearts:

> For although they knew God, they neither glorified him as God nor gave thanks to him, but their thinking became futile and their foolish hearts were darkened. Although they claimed to be wise, they became fools and exchanged the glory of the immortal God for images made to look like mortal man and birds and animals and reptiles (Romans 1:21–23).

The best antidote to this foolishness is a clear understanding of who God is.

In order to avoid the folly of worshiping the creature rather than the Creator, it is necessary that the individual also experience God's transforming work in his or her heart. Without that supernatural change that only God can bring, individuals will foolishly continue to worship false gods.

Therefore, it is absolutely essential that anyone reading this book reach a solid conclusion: that the information contained in the study is designed to direct people to recognize the need to have a proper relationship with the true and living God, as described in the preceding chapters.

God's Gospel

This book is about the God of the Bible, the God of traditional Christianity. He is a God who can be worshiped, adored, loved and served only by those who have experienced his life-changing work. That work of God is available to all who recognize that God has a right to claim their allegiance and their obedience. He made them, and continues to sustain them. He, therefore, can demand submission of all the people in the world. That is why it is important to realize that there is only one God, the living and true God.

Those who recognize that God has a right to make demands on them should also realize that they have not fulfilled those demands. All of us have failed to be the kind of holy people that God expects us to be. We have failed to be righteous, as he requires. The Bible clearly states that all have sinned and fallen short of the glory of God (Romans 3:23).

The study of who God is should have impressed on each reader the absolute righteousness and holiness of God. But as surely as we realize that God is perfect, just so surely must we acknowledge that we are far from holy. God justly requires perfection of people, and unless one recognizes that he is a sinner, he will not be able to understand who God is. God works only in those who openly confess that they have sinned against him and fully deserve his anger and punishment.

The supernatural work of God prevails in the lives of those who, having seen that they are sinners, also understand that God is loving and forgiving. Chapter 7 of this book dealt with God's love, and emphasized that the clearest demonstration of his love was shown in the redeeming work of Jesus Christ.

We can come to know and serve God only when we realize that there is no way we can rid ourselves of our sin, and that the work of Jesus Christ was for just such sinners as we. He who lived perfectly could satisfy for us God's demands for holiness of life. And because he was sinless, he was able to bear the punishment that our sins deserved. He did not suffer for his own sake—he suffered on behalf of all who trust in him.

The Bible calls people everywhere to recognize that God has a proper claim of obedience on all people. The message is equally clear that all should confess that they have failed to keep God's just requirements. And only those who realize their helplessness to meet them can understand what it was that Jesus did on the cross.

All who truly understand who God is will heed the call to put their trust in Jesus. Do you believe he can do for you what you cannot do for yourself? Do you trust that God will accept the work of Jesus to accomplish righteousness for you, and that Jesus bore your sins on the cross? Then you have experienced a birth from above and can understand who God is.

This is what it means to be a Christian—and only Christians can truly understand who God is. The supernatural work of God's Spirit in their lives enables them to comprehend some of what the Bible teaches about God.

Loving God

One of the ways in which we can increase our love for God is to learn more about him. As we do so, our love for him can increase as we meditate on who he is and what he does.

If you are married, you may have had an experience similar to mine. Sometimes when I travel, I begin to miss my wife. I will think about her, what she is like, how she acts, what she did and continues to do for me. Thinking about her makes me miss her all the more. But not only does that reflecting make me miss her, it also makes me love her more. I am filled with appreciation for her good qualities. I am moved to think about how little I have loved her in return. What impresses me is that as I think about her—her qualities and actions—I love her more and more.

The same thing can happen to us as we think about God. Meditating on God's character should lead the Christian to be filled with love for him. As we learn something new about him, we can meditate on that characteristic of his, and in so doing increase in our love for him. Just as this happens to me with regard to my wife, the same can happen to you in regard to God.

Thinking about God

People in the twentieth century rarely reflect or meditate—such an exercise isn't characteristic of the present age. Nevertheless, it is a significant tool in increasing our love for God.

You may ask, How do I meditate on God to the end that I will love him more? A good beginning is to recognize that the Bible is a book about God. That is why it is called "revelation"—it reveals God. The same can be said about the things that God has made; they reveal God.

When you look at the world about you, ask yourself what aspect of God's character is being shown to you. Paul was convinced that this was possible. "For since the creation of the world God's invisible qualities—his eternal power and divine nature—have been clearly seen, being understood from what has been made, so that men are without excuse" (Romans 1:20).

Get up before dawn some morning. Go outside and watch the sun rise in the eastern sky. See it as it peeks over the horizon. And then think about God. Those of you who are scientifically inclined will be aware that there are many fascinating phenomena occurring as the sun rises. For the poets among you, the beauty of the event will strike you. Visual images will be translated into thoughts and words. No matter what your inclination is, though, maintain a proper perspective on the rising of the sun: God is doing it. He is making the sun to rise in the morning as he has done for thousands of years.

No one else can do this. The scientist can explain it, and the poet describe it; but only God can make the sun rise. With that perspective in mind, remember that there is no other god. None other exists, so none can do the things that our God does.

As the sun mounts higher in the sky, think about what he is showing you about himself. He does make himself known— that beautiful sunrise is for you. It is for you to see, enjoy and revel in. But it is there most of all for you to see and to understand something about himself. In that sunrise, the heavens are declaring the glory of God, and you should be hearing their shouts of praise. Meditating upon God and his creation should lead you to love him all the more. Your remembrance that he is showing you something about himself should lead you to join with the heavens in declaring your love for the Creator, who is showing you his glory.

As the sun continues its ascent, look around you and see what is happening. Things that were just faintly apparent a few minutes ago are now clearly seen: the light of the sun opens new vistas for you. It makes it possible for you to drink in more of the fullness of the things around you. When that happens, think about the statement, "God is light, and in him there is no darkness." What you experience at that moment is only a small indication of what it means that God is light; nevertheless, you are privileged to savor a little more of God's revelation of himself to you. The darkness has faded, and you are feeling the warmth of the sun. As you bask in that warmth, reflect on all the things you now know about God as light.

The sun continues its climb into the sky; and as it does, think about its power. Without the sun, life would be impossible—it is the source of power for most life forms. If it should vanish, death would engulf everything on earth. But the sun will continue to rise and exert its power on the earth, so remember why the sun is rising. It is making its journey from east to west because of the power of God. Consider the power evident in this daily event, and then recall that God is doing this as a way of making his power known to his people—to you, his son or daughter. As you think about such things, will your love for God not increase? Will it not take on new dimensions of fullness?

As the sun rises, fascinating changes are taking place. People rise and go about their daily activities. The sun brought them to a state of wakefulness; the powerful light invigorates them and makes them ready to pursue another day of labor.

As I write, I can look out my window and watch a squirrel hurry by and a bird dart from a tree to the ground. I know these are creatures that work during the day. I also know that there are many nocturnal animals that were busy while I slept. And I, like you, am filled with wonder at the wisdom of God (see Psalm 104).

The sun will continue to rise, and you will continue to be caught up in wonder at the splendor of God. But take another minute to think about what is going on: God is making himself known to you. His world is once again functioning in the way he designed it.

Surely you will be filled with awe because of God's power and wisdom; but remember also his goodness. You sit there and enjoy all that occurs, and you can do so only because God is good. Take a moment to revel in God's goodness—stand up and awaken any late sleepers with a loud "Hallelujah!" The God for whom your love is growing deserves your shout of "Praise the Lord," for he is good.

You see, the knowledge of God that you have acquired can help you to love him more. As you think about what you know about him, you will be able to appreciate who he is and what he does. In so doing, your love for him will increase. You experienced the excitement of loving God as you watched the sun rise. Later you may enjoy a similar experience as you watch it set. Thinking and meditating on what you know about God will help you to love him more.

If you want your love for your great saving God to increase, take the time to reflect on his revelation to you in his created world. Find time to see the sun rise and set. Watch the way a small child grows. Think about the marvelous way your body functions. And as you do, keep in mind the things you know about God's character.

Not only can your love for him grow as you reflect on his work in creation, but the same can also be true if you think about his providence. Because God works everything out for the good of those he has called into his kingdom, reflecting on his care can help the Christian learn to love him more.

The process of meditating on God's providence was an important part of the ancient Hebrew poets' way of life. Look, for example, at the way the psalmist reflects on God's providence in Psalms 105 and 106. David also wrote in Psalm 69 about the issues that confronted him as he reflected on the providence of God.

Meditation on natural phenomena is not the only way we can learn to do so. The special revelation of God in the Bible also teaches us how to do this. But just like the things received through natural revelation, special revelation must also be used by the people of God in order for them to grow in their love for him. Psalm 1 explains the benefits of meditating on the Word of God. Christians who ignore this gift of God remain weak. Those who meditate on the Word day and night know how and why to love God.

God gives us a multitude of reasons why we should love him. He shows us how we can love him, and encourages us at every step to do so. If you want your love for God to increase, then you must avail yourself of the knowledge of who God is, and integrate that into your affections for the Creator of heaven and earth.

Learning to Serve God

God desires and demands that we love him. The love we render him should involve our whole being—our heart, mind, soul and strength (Deuteronomy 6:5; Luke 10:27). Those who learn to love God will also be zealous to serve him.

Rendering service to God can take many forms. We serve him when we gather together with the saints in worship. We also serve him when we engage in acts of kindness to those around us. Serving God is not something altogether different from loving him. Both functions are a part of what God demands of his people. But just as we need to learn continually how to love God, so too do we need to learn to serve him. Fortunately, the Bible helps us in innumerable ways to figure out how to serve God.

Worship and Service

One of the prime ways in which we serve God is in worship. The language of service is crucial to understanding worship in both Old and New Testaments. At the heart of Christian worship is the idea of giving to God the honor he deserves. When God's people do so, they are engaging in true service.

In the Old Testament, service was an integral part of worship. The ancient Hebrews were commanded to worship God by bringing him offerings of various sorts. It is interesting to note the way in which serving him in this manner also benefited others. For example, the priests were fed by some of the food offerings brought to God.

Early New Testament worship had some of the same focus. Worship was serving God; but in the offerings that were received on the first day of the week, the poor and needy also benefitted. People served God at Corinth by bringing their offerings, and at the same time the poor in Jerusalem were supported. So service in both Testaments was a part of worshiping God.

Why Worship?

Modern people don't think about worship as the first avenue for serving God. Nevertheless, we need to learn that God wants—and expects—our worship. He counts our worship as a part of the service that we should automatically render to him.

We worship and serve God because he deserves to be worshiped. If you have learned anything about the nature and character of God in studying this book, then you realize that God is worthy of worship. He deserves worship because he alone is God; there is no other. He is worshiped because of the marvel of his triune being. God, who is love, light and spirit, is to be honored with our hearts and lips. What response could be more appropriate for God's love, goodness, power, holiness and wisdom? Even those with a minimal understanding of God's nature and character recognize that he ought to be worshiped. Those of us who regularly learn more about him should also find ourselves desiring to render service to God through worship.

Service to God and Others

Not only does God want us to serve him, he also requires that we serve others. We show God that we know something of his love when we help the poor and needy among our brothers and sisters in Christ. Indeed, it is as we love others that we come to know that we are disciples of God.

The service that we render to others should not be viewed as something different or divorced from our service to God. He is pleased when his people reflect his love and goodness in their lives by serving others. In fact, it is in serving others that we will come to understand, in a fuller and deeper way, what God is really like. So service rendered to others in response to our understanding of the nature and character of God is service offered to God.

The God We Love and Serve

The title of the book you are completing assumes that God exists. Many Christians have difficulty recognizing who God is—there are so many other biblical teachings that they find more exciting. But the Bible is a book about God: it tells us what we need to believe about him, and what he requires of his people. The same is true of his revelation of himself in the world. Creation and providence both speak to us about God. In them he makes himself known.

Some people study about God to satisfy their intellectual curiosity. They are interested in learning about him because they enjoy being informed on various matters. Those who study about God for these reasons must be careful: he doesn't reveal himself to us simply to satisfy our curiosity. He makes himself known so that we can respond to him in loving service.

Others study about God because they want to know what he can do for them. They are interested in how God can help, encourage, or comfort them. These people also need to be careful—God does not exist for his people. The opposite is true: God's people exist for God. They exist to love and serve him. God *was,* and then he created a people. He made us for himself; he made us to serve him.

Christian men and women, those who have experienced the new birth, should recognize the multitude of reasons why God is to be loved. Those of us who have basked in his love in Christ ought to be clamoring for ways to love God more and to serve him more effectively.

As you close this book, remember who God is. Remember also that, because he is the kind of God he is, you are to love and serve him.

Review Questions

1. What have you learned about God from creation and providence?
2. What are some of the reasons people study the character of God?
3. How can you learn more about God?
4. What is the relationship between serving God and serving others?
5. What is at the heart of serving God?

Discussion Questions

1. Describe how you can—or do—meditate on God's character as you examine his creation.
2. Select a Bible passage that deals with God's character and explain how you would meditate on it.
3. How has your love for God changed recently? How would you like it to change in the future?
4. How can your knowledge of God help you to worship him better?
5. How do you plan to improve the service you render to God?
6. Describe the God you love and serve.